CX Trinity

Customers, Content, Context

*Musings and Observations on the Evolving
Customer Experience*

Alan J. Porter

CX Trinity
Customers, Content, Context
Copyright © 2015–2021 Alan J. Porter

Disclaimer

Credits

Cover design and illustrations: Douglas Potter

Trademarks

XML Press
Laguna Hills, California 92637
https://xmlpress.net

First Edition
978-1-937434-74-8 (print)
978-1-937434-75-5 (ebook)

Table of Contents

Foreword

by Cruce Saunders, Founder of [A] — simplea.com

Digital customer experiences are always mediated through content. And customers bring their own individual needs and environments to those interactions. More precisely, customers bring their context.

As Alan describes throughout the essays in this book, the CX Trinity emerges from this dynamic interaction of customer, content, and context. And this perception is exciting because it's the basis for a much bigger shift underway everywhere.

Moving towards intelligent customer experiences

For every retail experience, customers expect a counterpart e-commerce experience. For every customer service interaction by phone, customers expect an easier, more effortless online path to resolution. For every interaction with a salesperson, customers expect a coherent and usable online education and interactive sales funnel. For every offline process, there's an online counterpart. And, as customers, we all interact more with companies and experiences that feel smarter and more effortless.

We naturally gravitate towards smooth interactions that require less of our mental effort and time to engage. So, brand publishers need customer, content, and context to come together and assemble what [A] calls simply "Intelligent Customer Experiences."

In this new era we are building, we need to give customers:

- ► A coherent and holistic set of interactions across many journeys and touch-points stemming from within an organization.

- ► Highly relevant and streamlined interactions that come to meet them within their context, at their point of interest and need.

- ► Experiences that cross channels and devices seamlessly

The dawning of this new era of intelligent customer experiences makes incremental progress every day. The world is evolving to meet the needs of a growing and diverse population, all interacting and engaging across many devices in real time. Enterprises must pursue a major shift in the way knowledge moves around their organizations. We must get conscious about how content travels across departments, through systems, between creators, designers and developers, and into an ecosystem of devices and channels that is constantly and rapidly changing.

Embracing change

Every organization facilitates customer interactions that include digital communications in at least one channel. And some organizations engage customers across many content types and many channels. Keeping up with many channels is hard enough. Then we have to somehow make it all relevant to individual customers and groups of customers.

The personalized and fluid nature of this evolving reality has quickly rendered the old ways of dealing with static knowledge obsolete. The expression of an organization's products and services, support, resources, communities, and all forms of engagement, all rely on knowledge expressed as content, coming together in the customer's context.

The journey is just beginning

Even though customers have been at the center of digital experiences for more than two decades, in many ways all of us are still at the beginning of a journey. This next decade will realize a complete transformation in the nature of customer experiences and the way they are created.

This slow-burning transformation calls us to evolve our thinking and our collective action:

- ► We need to move beyond the static page-based and channel-based thinking that defined the digital customer experience up until now.

- ► We need to shift our thinking towards integrated, context-rich customer experiences built from a common, shared set of intelligent content.

- ► We need to aim for intelligent content that automatically assembles into customer experiences, driven by all the contextual data that businesses are so fastidious at gathering but not yet accomplished at using.

To get there, CX teams and enterprise publishing and knowledge teams need to embrace the complexity of this new era of engagement with the strategy, engineering, and operations necessary to make the complex look and feel easy and seamless to the customer.

Being part of the solution

During his tenure at [A], as head of content intelligence strategy, Alan Porter had a unique vantage point to observe the forward edge of this transformation through the lens of engagements involving many of the world's largest and most complex enterprise publishing environments. These clients cumulatively serve many billions of customer interactions every month across well-known digital properties.

As we collaborated together with these clients, we discovered and co-created the patterns, processes, organizational designs, and architectures that have helped shape how content gets acquired, managed, and delivered into customer experiences. These substantial CX publishing transformations all focus on creating content systems to support new interactions between customer, content, and context.

The transformations of content supply chains rely on lots of moving parts working together. And in every transformation, there is a champion. Someone who knows the issues today and sees the future. Someone who sees the new world of customer experience and who drives the vision for the changes needed to support that new world. And then, there are many others who join and become a part of the solution to the brokenness of content and customer experience.

Are you a part of the solution?

Join Alan as he surveys the customer experience landscape in this insightful and handy book of 52 accessible and idea-inspiring essays. And be a driving force towards smarter customer experiences!

Preface

Welcome to the *CX Trinity*, a look at how we talk to our customers, the content we provide for them, and the contexts in which they consume it. But before we start let's take a closer look at the title of this book. Why did I call it *CX Trinity*?

- **CX** is a regularly used abbreviation for *Customer Experience* and often used as a hashtag in various social media platforms when talking about the subject.

- **Trinity** comes from my belief that any good customer experience is driven by a combination of three thing:

  - Meeting the **customer**'s needs

  - Delivering the right **content** to help the customer

  - Understanding the **context** of where, when, and how the customer is interacting with you

That's why I divided this book into three distinct sections: Customer, Content, and Context.

The subtitle, *Musings and Observations on the Evolving Customer Experience*, gives a hint that what follows are personal anecdotes, encounters, and thoughts on what it means to be a customer in a rapidly changing world where the line between the physical and digital customer experience is continuously shifting.

These observations, ideas, and thoughts are pulled together in a collection of 52 essays that originally appeared as blog posts either on my Content Pool blog,[1] on LinkedIn,[2] or on the CMS Wire[3] website.

Why 52 essays? While you are more than welcome to read *CX Trinity* straight through, I realize that many of you are busy and maybe only have a few minutes to spare. So 52 essays means that you could set aside maybe 15 minutes or so once a week; grab a cup of coffee, tea, or other beverage; and have a year's worth of ideas to consume, digest, and maybe learn from. Or you could just dip in and try an essay on a subject or topic that's of particular interest at any given moment. It's up to you.

Whichever way you chose to consume this content, and whatever the context, I hope that you will enjoy the experience.

Acknowledgments

Although the idea of CX Trinity might have been mine, the end result is far from being a solo effort. As with any book project it can only be turned in to reality by a team of talented and helpful people. This one is no different.

In particular I'd like to give a shout out of thanks to my early readers, Mike Aragona and Mark Lewis for their insightful notes, ideas, and questions that helped the text be more focused.

As always, a note of thanks to Doug Potter, my regular XML Press cover artist (and sometimes comics collaborator), for another fun cover and the title-page illustrations.

I also want to thank my editor at CMS Wire, Siobhan Fagan, who has been patient and encouraging of my (almost) monthly contributions since 2016.

---

[1] http://thecontentpool.com
[2] https://www.linkedin.com/in/alanjporter/
[3] http://cmswire.com

Of course you wouldn't be holding this book in your hands, or reading it on the digital device of your choice, if it wasn't for XML Press publisher, and copy-editor extraordinaire, Richard Hamilton. This is my third volume for XML Press,[4] and it's always a pleasure to work with Richard.

Thanks also go out to Cruce Saunders of [A] for the excellent foreword and for sparking the idea of the CX Trinity in the first place.

Of course, the biggest note of gratitude goes to my wife, Gill, for putting up with the possibility that every shopping trip or travel experience can become fodder for one of my blog posts.

---

[4]The other two are: *WIKI* (Porter 2010) and *The Content Pool* (Porter 2012).

Introduction

"Know your customer" is one of the basic axioms of business. But how do you get to understand just who your customers are and what they want? Recently, we've tried to address that question using two methods: measuring "the voice of the customer" and capturing metrics that tell us where people are on the *customer journey*.

So let's take a closer look at those two methods:

The voice of the customer

What does voice of the customer actually mean? Let's start with what it isn't: capturing the voice of the customer is not about sending surveys and asking people to fill them in. Surveys are by their very nature self-selecting, and they only capture a point-in-time opinion of a small percentage of people, most of whom are already prepared to invest some of their time in your brand.

Social media monitoring might be a way to capture broader insights into what your customers think. It's flattering to know that you're being talked about (or maybe not in some cases), but again, this is mostly a self-selected cross-section of people who feel they have something to say about your brand and their experience with it.

Social media monitoring helps take a pulse of opinion, but don't place too much stock in the raw numbers. Numbers of clicks, likes, and similar measures by themselves are somewhat meaningless, but interpreted correctly they can be a useful way to show trends.

So what about measuring the actual voice when a customer calls the help desk or the support line? Remember those? Sentiment analysis of those calls can be useful, but it's an avenue that's fast disappearing as many companies try to deflect customers from using call centers or even having a voice at all.

All these metrics do is tell you what happened at a given point in time on some mythical customer journey that you made up.

The customer journey

Customer journeys are theoretical amalgams of the steps we believe our customers make when they interact with our brand. They are designed to help us model behavior and help us deliver the right experience at the right time.

But the reality is that every customer's journey and sequence of interactions with your brand is unique. You need to understand not only what they do and when they do it, but also why they do it.

Don't just measure, listen

So how do you answer the question of why someone does something at a given point? What drives the interaction with your brand?

Simple. Rather than just measure your customers, you need to really get to know your customers. It's a straightforward but old-fashioned idea: build relationships with them. Use the data you collect from your interactions not to make broad-brush, metric-based assumptions, but to reflect back that you actually understand who your customers are and what they want.

This may be old-fashioned in these days of big data, but nothing beats things like user testing, user groups, customer advisory boards, or getting on-site with a customer. Develop customer advocates and send them out with the sales, professional services, and support people. Put them in retail stores—you get the idea.

Sure, you can use tools like *artificial intelligence* (AI) and *machine learning* (ML) to spot trends in the data and evaluate metrics, but at the end of the day business is all about people-to-people interactions, and only we humans can provide the empathy and understanding needed to truly understand what our customers want, and why.

> So let's stop talking about the voice of the customer and the customer journey and start discussing the customer's story.

A new customer experience model

The traditional marketing/sales funnel and the associated customer journey maps were linear and ended at the point of acquisition, reinforcing the focus on obtaining new customers. As a result, the customer experience was also focused on building awareness and engagement leading to acquisition.

However, while acquiring a new customer is vital to any business, keeping that customer engaged and feeling valued can drive even more revenue.

Are you delivering a consistent, continuous digital experience for your customers as they interact with your brand?

Is that experience seamless as they move from mobile device to desktop website to eCommerce platform or even to a physical interaction?

Remember your customer's digital experience is the sum of the perception of each interaction they have with your brand, and any single below-par interaction can diminish that experience. This requires an enhanced understanding of the full customer journey, one that is an infinite engagement rather than a linear process.

The new model of the customer experience can be viewed from two different perspectives:

1. **The Customer Perspective:** A continuous experience where the customer buys and then owns (or uses) a product (or service) throughout its life cycle before repurchasing.

2. **The Enterprise Perspective:** A continuous process where the enterprise acquires and then serves a customer to lead to a level of engagement where it will acquire additional revenue from that same customer and/or more customers through recommendations.

The infinite engagement approach to the customer journey cannot be addressed by separate experiences at different parts of the process. To be fully effective, it has to provide an exceptional continuous experience that combines many different experiences, processes, and systems that all have to interact in a seamless way.

Investment in a strong continuous customer experience strategy will result in a customer becoming a brand and product advocate who will recommend the product or brand to others and who will want to build on the existing relationship through additional purchases and interactions. Instead of leaving the sales cycle, the engaged customer loops back into it.

Customers

customer (*noun*) plural: **customers**
cus·tom·er /ˈkəstəmər/

► A person or organization that buys goods or services from a store or business.
► **Similar:** shopper, consumer, buyer, purchaser, patron, client.

1

You Can't Predict the Future, But You Can Prepare

Growing up in England in the '60s, I was fascinated by a series of action-adventure TV shows produced by Century 21 Productions. The shows featured machines that traveled in space, underwater, or underground and performed fantastic feats or flew at tremendous speeds.

Then in the late '60s I came across a show called *Star Trek*, and I've been thinking about the future ever since.

My first job out of college was working on the Concorde supersonic passenger jet, and I also was tangentially involved with a project to design a hyper-sonic space plane.

Now here we are in the 21st century, and none of that happened!

Who can predict the future?

I love living in the future, although it's not the one I expected. We may not have flying cars and jet packs, but look at what we do have.

We all walk around with a pocket-sized device that connects us to the greatest repository of human knowledge in history. We can have instantaneous conversations across continents and use that same device to take photos, watch TV and movies, store and read a library of books, access the world's news organizations, socialize with millions of people around the world—and maybe even make the occasional phone call.

It's a technology that no one saw coming, yet in the space of less than a decade the smart phone has changed the way we live, the way we communicate, and the way we do business.

The times they are a-changin'

How can you possibly predict and prepare for a change like that? The answer is that you probably can't.

In the words of Nobel Prize winner Bob Dylan (and who would have predicted that?), "Something is happening here, but you don't know what it is, do you, Mr. Jones?"

But you can look at where today's trends and activities are heading and extrapolate.

One of the greatest moments of realization for me around how people interacted with content was watching my then 15-year old daughter doing a homework assignment on Pearl Harbor. When I passed her a book on World War II from my history bookcase, she ignored the table of contents and index and instead flicked through the pages until she found a photo she knew related to the subject she was studying. Only then did she start to read around it.

She did a visual search and then browsed the book like it was the web. At that point I realized that the traditional book paradigm no longer produced the user experience her generation needed.

Find the opportunities in developing trends

So what's happening now that will impact the near future? For the last decade I've been a big proponent of *augmented reality* (AR) as a way to communicate, engage, and inform. I believe it has great potential to deliver as yet unexplored customer experiences. I think AR will win over VR (*virtual reality*), because the latter is too immersive and isolating, but I could be wrong—the future will decide.

The best you can do is look at developing technologies and see how new generations use them. Extrapolate, and think about how that will impact your business.

Don't look for potential threats; look for potential opportunities. It's not about chasing the current hot gadget; the future is about recognizing change. Look outside your industry and outside your area of expertise. Get comfortable about being uncomfortable with new technology and trends. Study across many fields: technology, psychology, sociology, story-telling, movie-making, and more.

So how do you address the challenge of mapping the future? First, learn to recognize the future, and then be prepared to adjust when the jet pack turns out to be an iPhone instead.

Originally published on CMS Wire, November 2, 2016

2

Is B2B A Myth?

> Business-to-Business is a myth. Business is all
> about personal interactions.

These were a few words I added when I retweeted an article I'd read online that was headlined, "Don't hide behind a logo. Companies need to be represented by real people."[1] That small editorial addition generated some interesting response, most of which were along the lines of "B2B (*business-to-business*) is where the customer isn't the end user, while in B2C (*business-to-consumer*) they're the same."

These are reasonable definitions, but they don't address the central point I was making: whether they are buying something on behalf of a business, or for their own use, the customer is still a living, breathing person (I hope). It doesn't matter if you're buying office supplies or companies, it comes down to personal relationships and experiences.

A few days later I was listening to a business podcast where they were discussing a multi-billion dollar acquisition. Among the usual factors, such as a strong order book and good margins, one of the top reasons given for the deal going ahead was that the prime in-

---

[1]From cmo.com. However, a direct link is not available, and the site has no search capability

vestor "knew the CEO and the management team and how they operated." They had built a personal relationship that was driving perhaps the most quintessential of business-to-business transactions.

If you need new pens for your small business, which office-supply store will you go to? Most likely the one where you had the best experience last time you shopped there. The one where someone helped you look for what you needed, the person at the cash register smiled, and they actually knew your name and what your business does. Of course, it's the one that treats you as a person.

Or maybe you get your pens from a catalog that your employer says you should use. Why did that office-supply company become the corporate-approved supplier? Because their sales person got to know the people in your purchasing department and, therefore, was able to make a competitive bid at the right time.

The B2B/B2C distinction has always bothered me. Outside of work we are all consumers, yet there seems to be an underlying assumption that our behavior and expectations somehow change the minute we walk through the office door. I don't believe that.

Marketing content isn't (or shouldn't be) aimed at an organization; it's aimed at people within that organization. Good business marketing is about giving people information that helps them do their jobs better or makes their lives easier. It's about reaching decision makers: the people who can make a difference. Once again, it's people.

I have a content marketing best-practices list pinned up in my office and on that list is "Think human-to-human not B2B or B2C." I couldn't agree more.

Originally published on LinkedIn, September 8, 2015

3

Is Your Website a Reflection of You or Your Customers?

"Hey Dad, did you have any feedback?"

That text from my daughter was part of an ongoing discussion around the website she was designing for a new business venture that she and a partner were launching. It was the third iteration of the site, and this was the first version that was fully mobile friendly.

My feedback was that with just a few minor tweaks, this iteration was very close to where it needed to be for the launch. It told a good story and provided the basic information their customers would be looking for.

That wasn't always the case.

Early in the process of them developing a business case, I asked my daughter and her business partner what they wanted the website to communicate.

Their immediate response was, "We want it to let people know what we do."

A logical answer, but my response was something along the lines of, "That's great, but other people do what you do. What makes you special?"

"We are focused on people with a particular problem area."

"Great. So think about the people who need help solving that problem. What are they looking for?"

As discussions continued, the website design and prototypes evolved from a description of what the new company did to a series of short articles that addressed potential customer problems and how my daughter and her partner could help.

They also looked at the list of services they were offering and decided to focus on the three where they have the most interest. Now, instead of a web page with a shopping list of things to pick from, each solution article now has information about the relevant service, including pricing and contact information.

But it's not only small businesses and start-ups that need to switch their thinking from a website that, no matter how slick, is little more than a digital brochure. Often these *inside-out* websites end up being a reflection of the corporate structure accompanied by a list of products. Switching the mind set to a customer-driven, *outside-in* view can pay dividends by providing an improved experience that helps customers solve their problems. And it can also have a direct impact on the company's bottom line.

I once worked on a project for a large company whose website was a perfect reflection of their corporate and business unit structure. You had to know what part of the company was responsible for a particular product to be able to find it; even employees had a hard time figuring out where to find information.

A customer-focused analysis showed that 80% of the traffic went to the website for just four things: to look up product specifications, find pricing, buy spare parts, or get support. Once we rebuilt the website to make those tasks as easy as possible, traffic, leads, and online parts sales revenue all increased and support costs decreased.

Improving the customer experience is now regularly cited as a top strategic imperative for companies, and websites are central to that experience. Delivering a customer-driven web experience means focusing on what the customer wants from your website, not what you want.

Originally published on LinkedIn, June 21, 2017

4

The Fundamentals of Digital-Experience Project Planning

No one ever said implementing a new digital-experience project would be easy, unless they totally underestimated what is involved. Implementing a customer-centric digital transformation plan involves a lot of moving parts. Unfortunately, most of these projects quickly lose focus on the *customer-centric* part and become all about the *digital* part.

Let the experience drive the systems design

Managing the technology, although complicated, is in many ways the least challenging part of changing the digital experience. Looking at vendor demos, issuing requests for proposals, and running proofs of concept are easy ways to create the illusion that you are making progress on a project. However, putting technology first often means you end up either digitizing the existing process without making things easier for the customer or allowing system limitations to drive the experience rather than having the desired experience drive the systems design.

Avoiding the tool trap is easy. Don't allow yourself to start talking about technology and software until you understand what the real challenges are. What problems are you trying to solve? Why are there problems? What do those problems cost your organization? And what are you willing to do to make those problems go away?

Digital-experience project planning

When it comes to transforming the digital experience, the problems you need to solve aren't only internal problems, they are first and foremost your customer's problems. And only by exploring three essential aspects of planning a digital experience project will you truly address those problems.

1. Know your customer

I'm sure you know who your customers are. You probably know which of your web pages they visit, what white papers they download, and what products they buy. You probably also do follow-up surveys to find out what they thought of their interactions with your brand. And 90% of your customers probably ignore those surveys because surveys are about scoring your internal processes, not fulfilling customer needs.

You can't get to know your customers by examining how they interact with your existing processes. You need to discover why they do what they do and what problems they are trying to solve. The digital experience shouldn't be defined by what your products do, it should be defined by what your customers need.

2. Follow your customer

Customer journey maps can be a useful tool, and I'm sure we've all developed them. They help define strategies and approaches to delivering experiences. The problem with customer journey maps is that customers don't see them, and they don't always follow the nice routes we map out for them. Customers drop in and out of our theoretical maps. Typical customer life-cycles are made up of many, often disjointed, customer journeys.

While using techniques like analytics may help bring some of those disjointed journeys to light, the best way to truly follow customers is to walk in their footsteps and perform the tasks they do to solve their problems. By conducting a practical test of the digital experience, you can discover the bottlenecks and roadblocks that need fixing and identify opportunities to deliver additional value.

3. Understand your customer

Delivering real value to customers comes from examining the gaps between multiple, disjointed customer journeys. When customers aren't interacting with your systems they are elsewhere understanding and refining their needs, deciding what solutions or products can address those needs, and researching pricing, support, and related information that adds up to the total experience.

On one project I was involved with we interviewed over one hundred customers, asking them to walk us through what their job was (not how they interacted with our brand). We discovered most of them went through around thirty-five process steps between identifying a need and resolving that need. We as a company were directly involved in just eight of those steps. We knew a lot about those eight steps—we had all the analytics—but we knew nothing about the other twenty-seven.

Once we understood what the customer was looking to achieve through all thirty-five steps, we were able to provide valuable content to speed up the process. We also redesigned aspects of the digital experience with our brand to ensure we were asking for the right information at the right time to smooth interactions and make the overall experience as frictionless as possible.

At the end of the day, isn't that what delivering a successful digital experience is all about: making it easy for the customer to solve a problem or fulfill a need?

Originally published on CMS Wire, July 24, 2017

5

Great CX Starts With Trust: A Boxing Day Parable

"So what's this Boxing Day thing?"

During a break between sessions at a trade show in Chicago, I returned to my company's booth to be greeted with this apparently random question. As the token Brit on the team, it was assumed I knew the answer (and to be honest, it's a question I get asked at least once a year around the holidays).

May the strongest man win

"Boxing Day, which is celebrated in the UK and other Commonwealth nations, dates back to medieval times," I started.

There were a few nods of the head, and I realized my potential audience was hooked. So I decided to have some fun and spun a silly yarn about how the lord of the manor would select the strongest men from each of the villages on his estate. They would then engage in a no-holds-barred boxing match with the promise that the home village of the eventual victor would be spared paying any rents or taxes for the following year.

My poor colleagues believed everything I said … but I couldn't let it stay like that. After a few minutes, I confessed my bogus storytelling and described the true origin of Boxing Day.[1]

Trust and betrayal

My small, and short lived, deception got me thinking about trust. My audience trusted what I said because it perceived me as the subject-matter expert. The audience implicitly trusted me, therefore what I was telling them had to be the truth, especially because it sounded plausible.

In Chapter 23 I argue that it's OK to give the truth some scope (for example, an 11% increase could be termed double-digit growth) but any marketing claim must stand up to scrutiny.

So what about when interacting with the customer at other points along their journey?

Respecting your customers

At every point of interaction, the customer perceives you—and your employees, representatives, and partners—as being the subject-matter experts helping them meet their particular needs at that point in their journey. That role carries an implied trust that any information you give them (be it written, visual, or spoken) is current, accurate, and correct.

That trust should be respected.

---

[1]Oh, and the origin of Boxing Day? Although the first recorded use of *Boxing Day*, as applied to December 26, only dates from around 1830, it is related to the idea of a *Christmas Box*, which is thought to have originated in the 1600s. Traditionally servants in great houses were given the day off just after Christmas and would go to visit their families carrying boxes that contained gifts and sometimes leftover food from the celebratory meal at the great house. The term *Christmas Box* came to signify a gift given to a tradesman or servant during the holiday. Boxing Day has nothing to do with the sport of boxing.

There is nothing wrong with transparency. Not everyone can be expected to know everything about what your company does across all aspects of its operations.

By necessity, departments need to specialize. There will be times when you need to refer a customer to someone who is better able to provide the answers they seek. Such hand-offs should be as frictionless as possible, with the customer's data and interaction history seamlessly transferred from system to system or person to person.

It only takes one perceived falsehood to undermine the credibility of everything else that you do. It is better to hand a customer off to another expert than try to bluff, invent, or exaggerate just to resolve a customer question in the shortest possible time.

Great CX = trust + empathy

Delivering an exceptional customer experience is an exercise in empathy and trust. You must understand your customers, their needs, and the context within which they operate.

You must also respect the implicit levels of trust placed on you during every interaction.

Originally published on CMS Wire, December 5, 2016

6

Why You Should Deliver a Continuous Digital Experience

Are you delivering a consistent, continuous digital experience for your customers as they interact with your brand? Is that experience continuous as they move from mobile device to desktop to eCommerce platform or even to a physical interaction? Remember that your customer's digital experience is the sum of the perception of each interaction they have with your brand, and any single below-par interaction can diminish that experience.

Today most customers engage with brands through digital means. The digital world is driving a disrupt-or-die transformation. Allied with these trends is an increasing need for as many physical and virtual assets as possible to become digitized, intelligent, and incorporated into the end-to-end business process. One way to address this need is to look across your organization for opportunities to infuse great digital experiences into mission-critical processes.

Managing the way you engage with your customers ensures better customer experiences and helps build ongoing relationships. The customer is at the center of every business transaction, and keeping the customer engaged has never been more vital than it is now.

Traditionally, a new customer initiates a relationship at the recommendation or awareness stage and then cycles through defining a need, researching and evaluating a product, making a purchase, taking delivery, and using and maintaining the product. More and more of this interaction happens online, with the customer choosing to engage with a business only late in the sales cycle, if at all.

If the customer has little or no follow-up from the company or has a bad customer experience, they will probably move to a new supplier for any subsequent purchases, and you will have lost the opportunity for continuing business.

Investing in a strong customer engagement strategy and the technology to support that strategy will result in customers becoming brand and product advocates who will recommend the product or brand to others and will want to build on their existing relationship through additional purchases and interactions. Instead of leaving the sales cycle, an engaged customer loops back into it.

Positive customer experience is all about removing friction from the process. The easier something is to do, the better the experience. Customers increasingly expect transactions to seamlessly transition from one digital platform to another while retaining a consistent personalized experience with data, information, and assets moving seamlessly from one environment to another.

It is tempting to try to address this need by breaking down as many operational and silo-ed business and technology platforms as possible. However, this is often an impractical approach that leads to mismanaged expectations, delays, and higher than expected costs. It is better to create processes that allow data to flow between silos and build a suite of tools that works across silos.

Instead of trying to break down silos, bridge them into irrelevancy by delivering a customer-experience management solution that focuses on high-impact content (usually visual), strong transactional integration, and interactive customer communications and that allows you to conduct meaningful analysis to continuously refine the experience.

With an exceptional digital experience in place, it is not only your customers but also your supply chain, distributors, and employees who will benefit.

Originally published on LinkedIn, August 16, 2016

7

A Tale of Three Pubs: CX in a Culture of Assumption

An American walks into an English Pub wanting to order lunch....

It may sound like the beginning of a joke, but in fact on a trip I made back to the UK it proved to be a good lesson in delivering customer experience. Let me explain.

In an online exchange a while back a friend of mine used the expression "a culture of assumption" when describing her frustrations at dealing with various levels of bureaucracy after relocating to another country. People just assumed that she knew which forms to fill out and which agencies to contact.

I can totally sympathize, having gone through similar experiences when we relocated from the UK to the USA a couple of decades ago.

When we flew back to the UK for a family wedding, I noticed several examples of that culture of assumption on display—the unwritten, and probably unacknowledged, concept that your customers just know how things work when dealing with your processes.

From dealing with hotels to paying for parking to buying gas to checking in at the airport, there was an unstated expectation that we would just know where elevators were, where pay & display machines were located and how they worked, how to pay for gas at a pump that didn't have a credit card reader, or which check-in line to stand in and where to drop off our bags.

So back to the pub...

On three occasions over one weekend we went out with various family members for lunch at three different pubs. In each one we wanted drinks and a meal. After walking into the pub, we had to figure out what to do next, and in each pub the process was different:

- ► **Pub #1:** Find a table, note the table number, order drinks and food at the bar, and open a tab on your credit card. Food is brought to the table. Return to the bar after the meal to pay.

- ► **Pub #2:** Order drinks and food at the bar, pre-pay, get a number, and find a table. When the food is ready, your number is called, and you pick up your food at the bar.

- ► **Pub #3:** Order drinks at the bar, tell them you are eating, and be escorted to a table. A waitress takes your order and delivers the food. Return to the bar after the meal to pay.

Three pubs, three different processes, three different experiences. All of them were good meals, and I wouldn't want the pub experience to become a homogeneous standard—it's the differences that make the pub experience richer than the chain restaurant experience (especially in the UK).

However, none of the three pubs had anything posted to let you know how their individual lunch process worked. All it would take is a sign on or near the bar with a few steps explained.

Overall, the inconsistency in ordering pub meals doesn't seem like a big thing, but it got me thinking:

- ► How easy is it for customers to interact with your company?

- ► Do they have to know the way you work to achieve what they want, or do you make it easy with a guided customer experience?

- ► Do you assume that just because you know how to do something, that your customers (or even other employees) will?

Think of how your customers interact with your company and compare it to how you like to interact with other companies. Do you see any quick-hit solutions that could provide an easier starting experience? Do you have the equivalent of a "Press 1 for English" phone statement on your website?

Take the customer journey yourself and see if you get to what you need because you already knew what to do or because you were properly guided.

Originally published on LinkedIn, March 22, 2016

8

Are Your Customers Shouting Into the Void?

Many years ago I ran the support organization for a small software company. We had a whiteboard on the wall opposite the area of the office where my team sat. Everyone walking into the break room could see it. It showed the number of customer calls or emails we had each week, how many support tickets were still open, and how many we had resolved.

Above it sat another sign that said, "We are not a black hole."

Don't ignore customers
While the figures on the board were what we reported to the CEO each week, it was that simple informal sign that became our mantra. We didn't want our customers to feel as though their requests for service were disappearing into a black hole.

Let's face it: no one likes being ignored, but more often than not ignoring people is the standard operating procedure of many support organizations. Even if it isn't intentional, that's often the way it appears to the customer.

It used to be easy to monitor and listen to your customers. They either called, emailed, or even wrote actual letters (remember those?)

when they had problems. There was really no excuse for being a black hole and not responding to them.

Today, providing support is much a more complex undertaking. There are an overwhelming number of channels that customers can use to communicate with you, and while you may be able to monitor most of them, it is almost impossible to capture them all—especially when customers come up with new, unofficial channels to make themselves heard, like the gentleman who was so unhappy with a company that he painted his complaints on the side of a van.[1]

In my experience, companies respond to the voice of the customer in one of four ways:

1. Ignore it.
2. Capture it and do nothing.
3. Acknowledge there is a problem but take no action.
4. Acknowledge the problem and provide a solution.

Unfortunately, the response to any given request too often depends on when and where within the organization it was received and handled. This leads to an uneven experience. Companies do better when they treat customer input as a single unified data set.

Empathy first, followed by action

So how do you go about using that data set to deliver what the customer needs? The first rule of thumb goes back to not being a black hole. Acknowledge that the customer has a problem. Do that, and you'll be way ahead of most companies. However, while empathy is all well and good, customers prefer action to empathy.

How do you enable your teams to take actions that help customers? Give them access to *intelligent content*.[2]

---

[1]See Chapter 43 for his story.
[2]For more, I recommend *Intelligent Content* (Rockley 2015) by Ann Rockley, Charles Cooper, and Scott Abel.

Content is an expression of everything a company does, and it needs to be valued as an asset across a company. To solve customer problems and provide positive, actionable feedback, you need to be able to tap into that pool of content in efficient ways that allow the right pieces of knowledge to be pulled together to provide personalized responses.

That content can come from knowledge bases, technical documentation, support articles, operating schedules, customer profiles, or machine-learning chatbots. Match that content with current marketing campaigns and offers, and you can pull together positive customer experiences that help solve problems, further engage the customer, and continue to build brand engagement.

This comes down to taking a holistic, strategic view, this time in regard to your content. Look not only at what your content was created for but also at where else you can use it to answer customers' questions. That is not a quick or easy task, but it is one that increases efficiency, leverages your content assets, and allows you to respond to the voice of the customer in the best possible way.

Originally published on CMS Wire, February 1, 2018

9

Not Another @#$&! Survey

We all do it. Come on, admit it. I do it a lot.

You're at the store and while giving you your receipt (which is probably three times as long as it needs to be), the cashier grabs a pen, circles or highlights a QR code or website address, forces a smile (if you're lucky), and asks you to take a survey to "Let us know how we're doing."

Do you take those surveys? Probably not. I suspect that most people do what I do—toss the receipt in the nearest trash can.

Considering that I earn my living in the customer experience industry and like to think of myself as a customer advocate, it seems a little disingenuous of me to ignore those attempts to capture my voice as a customer.

Survey fatigue
The problem is that those sorts of surveys actually contribute to poor customer experience. Why should I provide a retailer with feedback and information that generates no tangible value for me?

I suspect that most customer surveys just add to a stockpile of data that no one looks at. This is just data collection for the sake of data collection, an exercise undertaken so someone can check the box when asked if the company has a program for capturing customer feedback. And when every retailer does it, the impact is the same as it would be if no one did. The surveys become meaningless. We have reached a point of survey fatigue.

Stop asking, start listening

When the average response rate to customer surveys tops off at around 10%, isn't it time to stop doing them? Or at least stop doing them the way we are? If we really want to develop effective strategies for capturing the voices of our customers, it's time to stop asking questions and start listening instead.

That doesn't mean that surveys can't be a useful tool. If used correctly, they can be a great way to start a conversation with your customers.

When engaged in a consulting gig, I often use surveys as a way to develop an understanding of how people feel and what works (or doesn't) with the processes and technology the organization is using. These surveys get response rates of 60% to 90% and provide a lot of useful insights.

Instead of blanketing a large group of people with generic questions, I target the surveys to discrete groups, with questions that relate to their day-to-day activities and that demonstrate an understanding of what the respondents are trying to accomplish and the challenges they face.

Surveys and voice-of-the-customer strategies should not just be about answering the question "How are we doing?" They should ask, "How can we improve things for you?"

Know the customer, help the customer

Every time you reach out to customers, you should demonstrate that you have listened well enough to know their needs and that you can help them. As a minimum, to demonstrate that you *know* the customer, tailor the conversation around the following topics:

- ► What products they use
- ► What interactions they've had with your organization
- ► What's important to them

Then you need to demonstrate that, if they provide you with feedback and share information, you can add value and help them in the following ways:

- ► Making their lives easier
- ► Reassuring them and/or directing to them more information
- ► Teaching them things that might be helpful
- ► Rewarding them

Gathering useful information and opinions from your customers requires you to do more than simply gather data. The purpose of the exercise should be to develop an understanding of their needs and challenges. By responding in ways that add value, you demonstrate that you understand your customers, which will help you capture their true voice.

Originally published on CMS Wire, March 4, 2019

10

The Ghost Map, Social Media, and Listening Outside

I highly recommend the book *The Ghost Map*,[1] by Steven Johnson, which details the story behind the 1854 cholera outbreak in London and the efforts of a few men, including the physician Dr. John Snow, to isolate the cause. Dr. Snow is perhaps most celebrated for developing the titular Ghost Map, which helped form a visual correlation between a cluster of deaths and the nearby contaminated water pump that turned out to be the root cause of the outbreak.

It's a fascinating book for anyone interested in social sciences, history, biology, and communication. A large part of the story discusses how Snow culled information from a variety of apparently disparate sources—some written, some verbal, and some his own observations—and brought them together to develop one of the most celebrated examples of technical communication and visual design of the modern age.

---

[1]*The Ghost Map* (Johnson 2006).

But the book itself has one great failing—it doesn't include a copy of the map! You know, the map that is referenced in the title of the book. The map that has a whole chapter devoted to it, and the map the author constantly refers to. A map that is in the public domain and widely available on the internet.

Here is a great example of setting up a reader expectation and failing to meet it. The quality of the content in this book is excellent, yet the one thing I remember most (and obviously decided to write about) was that single point of failure.

So how does this relate to corporate communications? Simply put: make sure that you deliver the content you promise, even if it's just an implied promise.

So to make sure I deliver on my own promise, what does the Ghost Map have to do with the social web? In the last two chapters of *The Ghost Map*, Johnson discusses the impact of Snow's work on science in general and the use of cartography in mapping social trends. In that discussion on maps he makes the following observation:

> The amateurs are producing the most interesting work, precisely because they have the most textured, granular experience of their community.

An astute observation and one that applies beyond cartography; it also applies to the changing face of corporate communications and social media. The day of experts being the sole trusted source of information is passing. As Don Tapscott and Anthony Williams put it in their book *Wikinomics*:[2]

> There are always more smart people outside your enterprise boundaries than there are inside.

---

[2] *Wikinomics* (Tapscott 2006, 45)

In London in 1854, the experts inside the organization (i.e. the government) were convinced that a mythical *miasma* was killing people. It took informed amateurs to identify the root cause and develop the documentation to prove their case.

Any organization today should be listening to, and encouraging, the participation of the smart people outside.

Originally published on LinkedIn, November 17, 2015

11

When Personas Go Wrong, or The Search for Fluffy

The woman on stage proudly told the conference audience how her team had spent three days to find just the right kitten for Emily.

Emily was a single working mother in her early 30s who lived with her 4-year-old daughter in a two-bedroom apartment. She was on a limited budget and often pressed for time. She also loved cats. Hence the search for the perfect kitten.

The thing was, Emily didn't exist. Emily was a *persona* dreamed up by the marketing team. The aim of the team was to create a series of recipes that used the company's products—a series of recipes just for Emily. And they spent (wasted) three days looking for a photo of a kitten to accompany a made-up person.

To be honest, I have a problem with Emily—and others like her.

Personas with too narrow a focus

By focusing on an individual as a persona you can narrow your focus too much and miss a large percentage of the customers and prospects who might benefit from your message.

By creating messages "just for Emily," the team was ignoring a wider need for anyone who wanted to create quick, nutritious meals on a limited budget. Personas should be focused on addressing customer needs, not on developing fictional characters.

It's a marketing point of view

Often, as with Emily, personas are developed by the marketing team with little or no interaction with actual customers. Marketing teams are often organizationally isolated from everyday interaction with customers, which can lead to personas that reflect what the marketing team thinks customers are looking for, rather than what customers actually need and how they go about finding information. It is essential that your marketing team take into account real-life customer experiences and needs.

Customers are changing

I have seen many personas documented along the lines of "Emily goes to the website to do initial research, checks reviews on mobile, and uses the app to purchase."

The customer experience evolves rapidly. I know my digital behavior patterns have changed over the last 12 months. You need to keep up with these changes. How often do you review personas to ensure that they keep up with new technologies and changes in how customers interact with your brand?

Still part of the "Sell and Forget" model

Historically, personas have focused on the buying behavior of a given set of potential customers. They were designed to drive people along the traditional sales funnel from awareness to lead to prospect to sale. But that only represents a small part of a customer's overall interaction with a company.

How do personas fit with the continuous customer journey?

Once prospects become customers they shouldn't be forgotten and neither should the relevant personas. How do your personas interact with your brand from delivery of the product through owning, operating, and getting support? Do you understand the full customer life-cycle of your personas and how their journey across every interaction with your company is connected and mapped?

Get that right and the satisfied customer persona can be your best advocate to generate even more business.

Was the kitten really necessary?

When you are developing needs-driven personas to help you understand customer behavior, your process needs to be systematic, efficient, and based on data. Building an emotional backstory for a character is all well and good if you are working on your latest novel, but it can be a time-consuming misdirection in developing effective customer-driven personas. How many customer interviews could that marketing team have done during the time it took to find the perfect photo of Fluffy?

Originally published on CMS Wire, February 6, 2017

12

Is Your Voice-of-the-Customer Program All Talk and No Action?

A hot and cold customer experience

On the way to a concert one evening, my wife and I stopped to grab a quick meal at one of our regular Tex-Mex fast-food restaurants. After patiently waiting in line, we got to the front and the server asked, "Can you wait a few minutes while I fill these online orders?"

I was not impressed with them giving priority to online customers over those who took the time and effort to be in the store, so I tweeted my displeasure. By the time we were sitting in our seats at the concert an hour later I had received an apologetic response from the company's social media team and a promise to follow up.

The follow up was an email on Monday with a generic "please rate your experience" survey attached. The good feeling created by the social media team's quick response was undermined by the apparent disconnect with the customer-service process.

Bland food, seasoned service

Contrast a few evenings later when I ordered delivery from another local fast-food chain. When the order left the restaurant, they emailed me a link to an interactive app where I could track the driver's progress towards our house. The food arrived ahead of schedule, hot and well presented with a print out on each container with the details of each individual order. But it wasn't as tasty as we felt it should be based on our in-store experience—none of the food had enough of the sauces that give the chain its distinct flavor.

The following day I had a survey call from them too. Not a generic email, not even a robocall automated survey, but an actual person who listened. When I mentioned the lack of flavor she said she'd pass it on. An hour later I had a call from the manager of the local restaurant asking for details of why we weren't 100% satisfied with the taste of our meals.

Guess who will get our service next time we want some fast food?

Stop asking and start listening

There's a well-worn saying that we have two ears and one mouth so we should listen twice as much as we speak. Too many companies use surveys to try and measure the customer experience, and in doing so say they are listening to, and capturing, the voice of the customer. But the truth is that these surveys don't really work.

As mentioned in Chapter 9, we all suffer from survey fatigue. Every single store on a recent shopping trip asked us to fill in a survey by going to a URL that the sales associate helpfully circled on the receipt. It sometimes feels as if you can't undertake any retail transaction these days without being surveyed.

How many do you fill in or respond to? I've seen and heard industry statistics that suggest that up to 90% of customer experience surveys are ignored. Why?

Some common reasons for low response rates include:

- Too many surveys from too many sources

- Too much time has elapsed since the customer's interaction

- Too much work expected from the customer (i.e. "Please go to this website and let us know what you thought")

- Nothing changes as a result of their feedback

The last point speaks to the heart of the problem: companies are collecting data, but they don't listen to what the customer is saying.

Analysis on voice-of-the-customer programs revealed that:

- 75% of companies collect or analyze data but derive few actionable insights

- 46% collect data but don't analyze or do anything useful with it

- 23% collaborate around this data with other groups

- Only 2% transform their business using collected data and the insights derived from it

The what and why of customer experience

How can you change that? First, acknowledge that there are two distinct types of questions you can ask to measure the customer experience: What? and Why?

What questions may be the best way to capture data. They include questions such as: What is your level of satisfaction? What is the likelihood you will recommend this product to others? Questions like this can tell you whether satisfaction with your customer experience is high or low, but they don't provide context.

Why questions provide context and sentiment: Why did this customer call? Why is that customer pleased or upset? Why, exactly, does this customer want to return, cancel, or upgrade?

In addition, there is interaction data, which includes open cases, phone calls, help-desk tickets, sales orders, or any other customer interaction information that gets recorded and tracked.

To derive the most meaningful insights from this data, companies not only need to understand the *what* and the *why* of customer interactions, but they also need to correlate the two. Customer experience managers need to take a holistic approach and consider both feedback and interaction data as one unified data set.

By taking a holistic view when measuring the customer experience, it becomes easier to identify and plan actionable changes. You can start from a single instance of a customer canceling service in a call recording and expand the data collection from there to view survey scores, *Net Promoter Score* responses, and other related feedback. Then, if the issue is compelling enough to merit a response that goes beyond dealing with that individual customer, it will be easier for you to define an action plan.

The start of a relationship

When customers know you are listening to them and that their feedback leads to measurable results and changes, they are more likely to continue to respond and develop an ongoing relationship.

After all, listening is the key to any successful relationship.

Originally published on CMS Wire, September 1, 2017

13

Are You Measuring Part or All of the Customer Experience?

A satisfied customer is a happy customer.

That's a well-worn saying—one that carries a degree of truth. But how do you know whether your customers are truly satisfied? Measuring something as emotional as an experience can be as much of an art as it is a science.

Why do people do what they do?

Sure, we have tools and metrics—surveys, *Net Promoter Scores*, the number of likes and followers—as well as behavioral analytics such as time-on-page and click-through and abandonment rates. And we use them to try and determine satisfaction levels. Although these metrics indicate what some people do, they don't tell you why.

Are your measurements tracking what you believe your customers want or what they actually need?

Customers don't come to your website or digital platform actively seeking out your latest marketing messages. They come because they have things they need to do. Those things can range from making a purchase to setting up an account to changing account information to paying bills.

Therefore, the success of a customer experience is measured by how easy it is to accomplish those tasks, not by how often users click your call-to-action buttons.

One area with a long history of helping customers get stuff done is the customer-support call center. In recent years, many companies are tracking the number of calls that get deflected from the support center to a self-help portal on their website as a metric of success.

But that doesn't measure customer-experience success; it measures a process change. If you don't have the right content on the self-help portal, and if that content isn't easily accessible and navigable, then you may be delivering a worse experience when you send people to the self-help portal.

The word *deflected* makes me shudder because it implies (at least to me) that the company doesn't want to engage with its customers.

Customers want answers

This is especially worrying when research shows that what most customers want when they engage with a company are answers to questions. For instance, research by the Search Engine Journal[1] showed that the top five content types that customers look for on a website can be summarized as follows:

- ► Answers to the five W's (who, what, when, where, and why)
- ► How-to guides or instructions
- ► Definitions (especially of complex terms)
- ► Product comparisons
- ► Prices and cost breakdowns

---

[1] "7 Types of Content That Dominate Position Zero" (Barysevich 2018).

That research confirms that customers want easy access to answers from any part of your organization. It's no longer true (if it ever really was) that marketing provides one type of information and customer support provides another.

In the business-to-business environment, there is strong evidence that customer-experience needs are driving cross-functional convergence of content. IBM Digital Analytics reported[2] that over three-quarters of the visitors to its main websites want to look at technical content about the use and implementation of its products. Therefore, they now include metrics for what were traditionally seen as a support functions in their overall customer-experience reporting.

Take a holistic approach

Are you measuring in isolation as opposed to holistically?

In general, the metrics used for measuring customer experience still tend to be the indicators of success (or failure) for individual operational departments or groups. Rarely, if ever, are they looked at in a holistic way to provide an overall measurement of customer satisfaction.

It's possible that you could be scoring highly in specific categories but still delivering a poor overall customer experience because the journey is disconnected.

By looking at customer-related metrics as part of an overall ecosystem and not as separate performance indicators, you can develop a clearer picture of your customers' overall journey.

Originally published on CMS Wire, September 6, 2018

---

[2]Personal communication with Andrea Ames, CEO/Founder @ Idyll Point Group.

14

Stop Using Customer Metrics to Live in the Past

Admit it, we all do it. I'm talking about how whenever we post something online, we can't help but check back later to see how it was received. Thumbs up, likes, retweets, comments, downloads, page views. We all love metrics, whether it's just "did anyone like the picture of my cat I posted on Instagram yesterday" all the way up to complex reports about web traffic, journey flow, click-through rates, and all that good stuff it takes a data scientist to sift through. We have so much data available about customer interactions that the true meaning is often forgotten.

The problem is that most metrics record what someone did in the past—typically an interaction with your content by either clicking a button or following a link. They don't tell you why the person did what they did.

And knowing why is the most important part of understanding the customer journey.

Getting to the *why* (and *why not*) of customer behavior

There is an excellent video from Adobe entitled *Click, Baby, Click*[1] that shows how reacting to clicks without knowing what is driving them can lead to an incorrect interpretation of customer demand. If you haven't seen it, I highly recommend watching it—it's a fun lesson you won't forget.

So if action-based metrics don't provide the information you need, do time-based metrics give a better picture of what drives customer behavior? They are probably a step in the right direction, but they have the same underlying issue—they still reflect past action. You may now know how long someone interacted with your messaging but not why.

For instance, time-on-page can be a false indicator: is someone engaged because your content is good and they enjoy reading it, or is it so obtuse that they have to keep plowing through it to find the answers they want?

Most people come to websites or interact with apps for one of two reasons: to get answers to questions or to complete a transaction. So maybe we should be measuring how well we achieve those two things. Instead of using page-based analytics, shouldn't we focus on content and transaction-based analytics combined with search analysis and time reporting to determine how easily, or quickly, customers achieve their goals?

On top of wanting to know what people do during a customer engagement and why they do it, it's equally important to know why someone didn't do what you wanted them to do. Why is no one clicking on that beautifully designed call-to-action button? Why isn't anyone finding the high-value content that would help them? This is where tools like *heat maps* can help you track where people engage with your designs.

---

[1] https://youtu.be/N1ltwg2nTK4

Understanding intent

So if the current metrics are a snapshot of past physical actions, how do you realign for a future where interactions migrate from the physical to the digital or to even more esoteric forms of interaction?

Think about the growing use of voice-based assistants such as Siri and Alexa. How will you measure audio interactions?

In many ways we already do, but for a different need. When you call a telephone helpline or get passed to a call-center representative with a message that says "your call may be recorded for training purposes," chances are high that training is low on the list of reasons why the call is being recorded. Call centers have long used technology to record, index, and analyze customer interactions not just for what was said, but also for tone and inflection.

Sentiment analysis may drive the next generation of metrics for voice-assistant-driven interfaces, not only allowing you to understand what a customer asked for and wanted, but also, with the application of machine learning, allowing you to start to understand not just how someone feels about an interaction but also what it was they were hoping to achieve in the first place.

Once you understand intent, as opposed to past actions, you can start to deliver predictive customer experiences and look forward instead of backward.

How can we help you?

The only true indication of a successful customer experience is whether you helped the customer do what they needed to do in a quick, intuitive, and helpful way. Did you make their day easier or answer their question? The more you remove friction from the customer experience, the more likely those customers are to return and want to engage with you again.

Originally published on CMS Wire, May 2, 2019

15

The Future of Customer Experience? Ask a 3-Year-Old

If there's one person I'm learning a lot from these days, it's my 3-year-old granddaughter. Watching young Hazel encounter and learn to navigate her way in the world is a delight and incredibly instructional. She has no preconceived ideas of how things should work, nor does she have any built-in assumptions of what an interaction should be. She learns by copying and, most of all, by trying: pushing her limits of what is socially acceptable, and technologically feasible, to help her obtain her goals.

Hazel is the best predictor of the customer experience.

Goodbye keyboards, hello voice?

Very early on she figured out voice assistants. If she sees a phone laying on the table, rather than pick it up she will shout at it—and make no mistake, she expects an answer. She loves listening to Siri and will babble away at the phone for a while. Watching her made me think there's a strong possibility that as she grows up she may never need to touch a keyboard. Will all her digital experiences be voice-driven?

Certainly more and more of mine are. I no longer write (or type) a shopping list, I just tell my phone when I've run out of something and it gets added to my shopping list. I access my most commonly used notebooks with a voice command, I check the weather each morning with a sleepy command from deep beneath my comforter before rolling out of bed to tackle the day. I use voice commands in my car, and at home I talk to a little black box to play music, control the heating system, play music, and even sometimes to turn on the TV and find the program I want to watch.

With the rapid adoption and increasing number of voice-activated interfaces, it seems that it is indeed the future of customer experience.

Unless you have an accent.

I'm a Brit living in the US. And it appears that the current generation of voice assistants still have a way to go in dealing with inflections, phrasing, idioms, and patterns of speech that fall outside of fairly narrow parameters. I've heard similar frustrating stories from friends with a variety of accents ranging from Polish to Scottish to Norwegian to Japanese. All of them speak excellent, clear English, yet they struggle to be understood by US-developed voice assistants. Localization of the technology is still a missing ingredient.

Voice technology: like second nature
Given the rapid development of voice technology, I view the accent issue as a short-term obstacle. Voice recognition and voice-driven interaction is here to stay and will only keep growing.

Why? Because it's the most natural way of communicating we have. Talking and listening have always been how we communicate—before computers, before TV, before print, before written scripts, and even before cave paintings.

There's a biological reason why voice assistants are so engaging. On average we type at around 40 to 80 words per minute and read at 250 words per minute, but we both speak and listen at around 130 words per minute. So conversational voice-driven user interfaces feel the most intuitive because the speed of delivery and processing are naturally synchronized.

A final (surmountable) challenge

If anything is holding back the speed of adoption of voice assistants in the user experience realm, it's engineering the content to feed it. At the moment, most assistants perform specific functions based on programmed keywords (and you only have to enter that keyword slightly wrong to experience some baffling results), or they input that command into a general search query and return best-guess answers, often with a "is this what you were looking for" modifier. We are some way from having a true interactive question-and-answer response paradigm because very little content is currently produced with that paradigm in mind.

Artificial intelligence systems (such as voice assistants) need modular content to be successful. When we get that right, I believe we will see an exponential rise in the use of voice interfaces that will transform the customer experience in a way that young Hazel will just take for granted.

Originally published on CMS Wire, January 31, 2019

16

Redefining The Customer Journey

Management consultant and author Peter Drucker once wrote that "the purpose of a business is to create and keep a customer." This may seem obvious, but many companies focus on the first part of that statement to the detriment of the second part. I would argued that keeping a customer is more important than finding a new one, because a repeat customer is often an engaged customer.

The digital world gives you more ways to know your customer better. Knowing your customer has become a key competitive differentiator. The best way to satisfy your customers is to truly understand them. You can do this by mapping your customer journeys.

But customer journeys are always changing. The old traditional model of a singular, pre-determined linear path or funnel from awareness to purchase no longer applies in a digital world where flowcharts have given way to multiple interactions wherever and whenever the customer wants them. Customers not only drive when and how interactions are made, they also want those interactions to be personalized.

In an article on CMS Wire,[1] John Zimmerer outlined a vision of a digital-experience platform that delivers "individualized content presentation for each customer interaction." To achieve this vision, organizations need to find better ways to engage with customers. This requires an enhanced understanding of the customer's journey—one that is an infinite engagement rather than a linear process.

The process can be viewed from two different perspectives:

► **The customer perspective:** a continuous experience where the customer will *buy* and then *own* (or use) a product (or service) throughout its life-cycle before repurchasing.

► **The enterprise perspective:** A continuous process where the enterprise will *acquire* and then *serve* a customer, leading to a level of engagement where the enterprise will acquire additional revenue from that customer and/or more customers through recommendation.

The fully engaged customer journey cannot be addressed by separate applications at different parts of the process. To be fully effective, it has to provide an exceptional continuous experience made up of a combination of many different experiences, processes, and systems that all have to interact.

These different aspects of the journey can be grouped into separate, but interdependent, layers:

► The customer's activity
► The company's activity
► The departments involved
► The metrics used to measure and manage the engagement

These four layers will be discussed in more detail in the following four chapters.

Originally published on LinkedIn, August 30, 2016

---

[1]"From Here to Infinity" (Zimmerer 2016).

17

The Redefined Customer Journey: The Customer's Perspective

The digital customer journey is being redefined. It's never been easier to buy stuff; all it takes is a few clicks of a button. But there are an almost infinite number of websites and online sources from which to make purchases.

How do you choose? In today's digital age do you simply buy something or do you create ongoing relationships with the companies that meet your needs and provide a good experience? I'm guessing that it's probably more of the latter.

The customer journey is being redefined in the digital age from a linear process to an ongoing loop of *buy* then *own* with the companies you choose to deal with becoming more and more engaged in every part of the cycle.

But what does that on-going loop look like from a customer perspective? Although the experience is continuous, it has ten stages:

1. **Awareness:** Do you know what is available in the market place that relates to your activities, business, or lifestyle?

2. **Need:** Why do you buy something? Generally, it is to fill a business or personal need. Does it solve a problem, make life easier, or just provide pleasure? Defining a need is an essential part of the purchasing process.

3. **Research:** Once you identify a need and match that need to an awareness of what is available, you often start to ask questions. What have others used or purchased to meet a similar need? In the digital world, research plays a more and more important role with the majority of purchasers doing their own research rather than engaging with a sales person to get answers.

4. **Evaluate:** How do various products and solutions compare? What are other people's experiences using them? The collective experience of peer groups is becoming a vital part of the evaluation process in a connected social world.

5. **Buy:** Once you have made a decision, the ideal purchase experience should be frictionless and consistent irrespective of which channel you use to make the purchase.

6. **Delivery:** This is the point where the experience moves from the *buy* to the *own* part of the process, and it is often the point where companies step away from a relationship with the customer. Delivery, be it digital or physical, should be well documented, well communicated, and as fast and efficient as possible.

7. **Use:** The everyday use of a product or solution is the longest part of the customer experience, and yet it is often the most overlooked. How easy is it to actually use what you have purchased? Does it meet your needs and expectations? Does the company you purchased it from provide information on its continued use or ways to connect with other customers to compare experiences?

8. **Maintain:** What if something goes wrong? How easy is it to get help or receive product updates?

9. **Advocate:** Do you talk about products, services, and solutions that you enjoy? So will your customers. Customers who have a positive experience will become brand and product advocates.

10. **Recommend:** Good advocates will recommend to others. Or they will self-recommend and make repeat purchases based on having been engaged as part of a well-designed and delivered continuous journey.

The fully engaged customer journey cannot be addressed by separate applications at different parts of the process. To be fully effective, the customer journey must provide an exceptional continuous experience made up of a combination of the many different experiences and processes.

Originally published on LinkedIn, September 23, 2016

18

The Redefined Customer Journey: Questions to Ask

In Chapter 16 and Chapter 17, I talked about the way the customer journey is being redefined in the digital age from a linear process to an ongoing loop of *buy* then *own*, with the companies you choose to deal with becoming more and more engaged in every part of the cycle. I've also discussed what that ongoing loop looks like from a customer perspective. But how does this relate to the activities within a company to support that experience?

An important part of the redefined customer journey loop is considering how your customers' activities map to those of your organization as you attract, inform, teach, and convert customers and then follow up with logistical operations, on-boarding, and ongoing support. Winning organizations also use engagement assets, such as loyalty programs, to up-sell and cross-sell to existing customers, thereby generating revenue at a lower cost of sales.

Although the overall experience is continuous, it is made up of eleven distinct stages:

1. **Attract:** Before you can build any relationship with a customer, you must first make potential customers aware of the company and attract them to find out more. Do people in your potential market know you exist?

2. **Inform:** Your company should then inform potential customers about the products and/or services you offer. It's surprising how many companies miss this step and just rely on building brand awareness without actually telling customers what they do. What is it that you do?

3. **Learn:** Another step often overlooked is learning about the potential customer. In today's digital world customers expect a more personalized experience and service that meets their particular needs and requirements. Do you know who your customers are and why they need your products?

4. **Convert:** Perhaps the key moment of the customer journey is the transition from prospect to customer. Ensuring that the previous three steps have been well executed can ease the conversion process. Unfortunately a lot of companies focus on conversion and see it as the culmination of the process when, in fact, it is the start of a potential ongoing relationship that can drive more revenue.

5. **Transact:** How easy is it to do business with your company? Personally I've dealt with too many companies that make it difficult for me to give them money, and many of those companies lost my sale. The easier it is for customers to complete a transaction the more likely they are to want to repeat the process.

6. **Logistics:** Once your customer has paid for your product and/or service how do you deliver the goods? Is it a quick frictionless process, or is it a long drawn-out experience?

7. **Onboard:** How do you make it easy for your customers to set up and start using your product? Do you welcome new customers to your company and community?

8. **Support:** Supporting your product is not just about helping to fix problems, although that is an essential part of it. Do you make it easy for your customers to own and operate your product? Do you connect with them on a regular basis? Do you use analytics and trends to be proactive with your customers? You should be supporting the customer, not just the product.

9. **Loyalty:** How do you make your good customers into great repeat customers? Loyalty programs are one good way to do that, but you need to prove that they benefit your customers as well as the company.

10. **Up-sell:** Do you understand your customer's needs well enough to anticipate when they need to upgrade to the latest version of your product?

11. **Cross-sell:** Can you identify what other products from your portfolio will help your customers meet their business or personal needs? Do you know how to attract their attention and inform them about those other offerings? Have you built a solid ongoing relationship that means you can continue on the customer's journey together?

I believe that this layer of the customer journey is best summarized in a tweet from Mark Hurst, the Founder and CEO of Creative Good:

> Did you know that your company has a team responsible for managing the customer experience? That team's name is 'the entire company'

Originally published on LinkedIn, October 6, 2016

19

The Redefined Customer Journey: The Departmental View

The customer journey is being redefined in the digital age from a linear process to an ongoing loop of *buy* then *own*, with the companies you choose to deal with becoming more and more engaged in every part of the cycle. As we dig deeper into the journey map it's time to highlight the various departments involved in the ongoing customer engagement model. It is no longer sufficient to leave customer relations to the sales or support groups.

Customer experience is now a mission-critical, cross-functional activity. As Robert Rose of the Content Marketing Institute often observes:

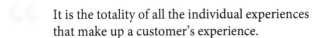 It is the totality of all the individual experiences
that make up a customer's experience.

Although responsibility for customer experience and the customer journey belongs to the company as a whole, in practice responsibility primarily falls within the following areas: marketing, sales, finance, distribution, operations, services, support, and customer care.

Delivering and supporting a positive customer experience is all about removing friction from the process. The smoother the transition from department to department, the better the experience. This means that each department should invest in the overall customer experience, including systems, training, education, and customer advocacy.

Serving your customers across a continuous digital experience maximizes customer life-cycle value and increases revenue potential.

The more other departments invest and buy in to the overall concept of a frictionless process, the greater the experience and the greater the customer's investment.

The benefits from committing to a combined, systematic approach to growing customer lifecycle value across the enterprise include:

- ► Increased customer retention rates

- ► Increased customer satisfaction scores

- ► Increased revenue

If you take this a step further by managing and delivering outstanding customer experiences, you will drive benefit for the customer as well as sustainable growth across the enterprise.

Originally published on LinkedIn, October 24, 2016

20

The Redefined Customer Journey: Measurement

"You can't manage it if you don't measure it," has been a business cliché for decades. It's not a sentiment everyone agrees with—not everything worthwhile can be measured—but measurements can provide useful insights into trends and behavior patterns.

So how does measurement (or lack of it) relate to the redefined customer journey?

In previous four chapters I looked at different aspects of the customer journey: the customer perspective, company activities, and the departments involved.

This article examines how to measure and manage the return on the investment in a continuous customer engagement strategy by linking *key performance indicator* (KPI) metrics to different stages of the engagement.

Typical KPIs used to manage stages of the customer journey include the following:

- **Net Promoter Score (NPS):** A calculation based on responses to a single question: How likely is it that you would recommend our company/product/service to a friend or colleague? The scoring for this answer is most often based on a 0-to-10 scale with anomalous outlier scores discarded.

- **Revenue:** The income that a business has from its normal business activities, usually from the sale of goods and services to customers.

- **Total Cost of Ownership (TCO):** Usually a summation of the total cost to your customers to acquire and operate the product plus any costs related to replacing or upgrading the product at the end of its useful life.

- **Return Rate:** Usually expressed as a percentage of the number of products sold that are returned.

- **Call Resolution Time:** The elapsed time between a customer reporting a problem and the issue being reported as resolved. Most support groups have target resolution times, which may vary depending on the customer's contractual status.

- **Churn:** The proportion of contractual customers or subscribers who leave a supplier during a given time period. It is a possible indicator of customer dissatisfaction or issues with the overall customer experience.

- **Likes / Impressions:** Usually a collection of web and social media metrics such as: page views, followers, and the number of posts that receive comments, likes, or are shared online. All of these metrics contribute to an overall *brand equity*, which measures how customers perceive the overall brand, its promise, products, and their experience.

This is not an exhaustive list. You may be using other KPIs to measure and manage customer interactions. Most companies use KPIs to indicate success (or failure) for individual operational departments or groups.

However, rarely, if ever, do companies look at them in a holistic way to provide an overall measurement of customer satisfaction. It's possible that you could score highly in individual categories, yet still deliver a poor overall customer experience due to a disconnected journey.

By looking at customer-related metrics as part of an overall ecosystem rather than as separate KPIs, you can develop a clearer picture of a customer's overall journey.

Originally published on LinkedIn, February 20, 2017

Content

content (*noun*) plural: **contents**
con·tent /ˈkäntent/

- ► The material dealt with in a speech, literary work, etc., as distinct from its form or style.
- ► Information made available by a website or other electronic medium.
- ► **Similar:** subject matter, subject, theme, message, material, ideas, text, images, video.

21

This Song Isn't About You

> Marketing is about *telling* the world you are a rock star; content marketing is about *showing* the world you are.

This quote is from my friend Robert Rose of the Content Marketing Institute, and it's easily the most repeated phrase I use when I am introducing the concept of *content marketing*. In fact, I like it so much that I had a poster made with that quote and have it hanging on my office wall.

It appeals to me on several levels, not least of which is that I'm a rock music fan and occasional historian with a particular interest in the early days of rock 'n' roll.

Robert's right that traditional advertising and marketing is about putting on a glitzy show in the hope that potential customers will notice. We have built a whole industry and profession around shouting "Look at me!" and singing songs about how great we are. But when everyone is singing the same words to different music, you get a raucous din in which everyone's message is lost.

The only way to cut through that noise is to stop singing about yourself. Instead, it's time to start singing about the things that help your customers achieve their dreams.

I developed a mission statement for how to deliver marketing content that hangs on my office wall right next to Robert's quote:

> We will provide *engaging, relevant, actionable* content that provides *value* to our customers, enabling them to be successful in reaching their business goals.

You need to make sure that the song you are singing shows your customers that you understand their business goals and needs.

Originally published on LinkedIn, June 23, 2015

22

Content Marketing Is All About Pain

I hate the gym. I'm happy to admit that. I've never considered myself to be any sort of athlete, and I find working out just for the sake of exercise boring in the extreme. As for pain, I'm a total wuss; I don't like any sort of pain, so the tried and trusted mantra of "No Pain, No Gain," has always been something of an anathema to me … with one exception: content marketing.

You need to feel pain in business. Not physical pain, but the pain of delivering what you are in business to do. While overcoming your own business pains can indeed help you grow, that's not the most important pain to consider.

> The pain you should be considering, especially when it comes to content marketing, is your customer's pain.

Your company, no matter what its size, exists to solve problems with its product or service. You are in business to fulfill a need, and that need is your customer's need. You drive revenue by making sure that you meet that need by solving the problems and pain points that stop your customers from being successful in their business and meeting their own customers' needs.

Often as companies grow they lose sight of the customer and become more internally focused, especially in areas that don't have direct contact with customers. When that happens, traditional marketing starts to be more about messaging how great they are and not what they can do to help their customers.

Content marketing changes that.

Content marketing is about providing value to your customers to help them succeed, and to do that you need to know their pain points and focus on delivering the information, knowledge, and inspiration to remove that pain.

If you want to make business gains, then you need to start feeling some pain. Just make sure that the pain you feel is your customer's pain. Then become the trusted source to ease that pain.

Originally published on LinkedIn, July 8, 2015

23

Truth in Marketing is not an Oxymoron

I'm a writer; I take the truth and give it scope.
—Paul Bettany as Geoffrey Chaucer[1]

If I have one underlying tenet that I try to live by, it's to tell the truth. It's a philosophy I also apply to my writing. Most of my published work to date has been non-fiction, which by its very nature involves a lot of research and fact checking to make sure that what you are presenting is the truth.

The problem with doing research based on historical events, particularly in the case of biography, is that the *truth* is often what the person telling the story believes to be true. For that reason, as much as possible, I try and go back to original sources and documentation.

The same thing applies when I'm writing fiction, I always try to stay truthful to the established rules of the fictional world I am working in. With a licensed property—where you are writing within an existing fictional world, such as the *Spider-Man* franchise—that also means doing a lot of research into the facts that other writers have established.

---

[1] *A Knight's Tale* (2001)

So what has this got to do with marketing?

Over the years I've written a lot of marketing communications: blog posts, Twitter, white papers, product literature, websites, promotional comics, and press releases. And, as with my other writing, I always try to tell the truth. Sure, as the quote at the start of this post mentions, I sometimes take the truth and give it scope. I'm perfectly happy saying that 11% is double-digit growth or that 51% equates to most because, beneath the spin, they are still verifiable facts.

Where I have problems is with marketing spin that uses absolute terms like unique, best-ever, ultimate, or first. If you want to use those terms, that's fine—but do some research and fact checking to make sure that you really are the first to market or that what your product does really is unique. And if what you are offering really is the ultimate, does that mean you will never improve it?

Say the wrong thing or use the wrong word, and there's a good chance someone will check, and if what you claim isn't true, they will call you out on it. That will undermine every other marketing message you put out.

> One perceived falsehood can undermine the credibility of everything else you do.

Oh, and one more little thing that drives me crazy. If you refer to another company or one of their products by name—whether in a press release, article, or any communication—make sure you get the name right. In this day and age, fact checking has never been easier; all it takes is a few clicks of the mouse.

There is no excuse for any marketing material not to tell the truth. Sure your readers may have to read between the lines or decipher the spin, but the foundation of what you are saying should always be verifiable.

Originally published on LinkedIn, October 6, 2015

24

How to be Arnold, Not Mary-Kate (or Ashley)

> Why be Mary-Kate and Ashley when we can be the Arnold to the rest of the industry's Danny DeVito?

It may sound like a strange conversation, but it's one I've had several times at different points in my career, usually when I've been at small- to medium-sized spin-off or start-up software companies. The underlying conundrum behind the question was "How do we differentiate ourselves?"

Nearly every business, to a greater or lesser extent, is akin to a commodity-driven business these days. There are very few disruptive companies whose success is solely because they are the only one doing something. Everybody has a competitor or two, or lots, all doing essentially the same thing, especially in a global marketplace.

If someone tells you what line of business they are in and you answer "Me too," then you are a commodity. If you don't differentiate yourself through the unique value you bring to your customers you become like Mary-Kate and Ashley Olsen on the sitcom *Full House*, where the two twins played the same character—a product that can be swapped out with one that does basically the same thing.

So how do you differentiate your value?

With CONTENT

Content can make you stand out like Arnold Schwarzenegger towering over Danny DeVito in the movie *Twins*.

Look at what makes your company and products special. What value do you provide that helps solve your customers' problems? What unique perspective can your company provide? What can you learn from your company experts and your customers?

If you find a niche where you can provide the most informative, engaging, and useful information, then plan to become the industry's leading expert in that space.

With the right content and the right approach you can position yourself to tower over others who may think they are just like you.

Remember—Be Arnold, not Mary-Kate (or Ashley).

Originally published on LinkedIn, August 11, 2015

25

Do you know your Brand's Origin Story?

I'll confess, I love origin stories. They are among the storytelling tropes that first attracted me to comics, and over the years I've even written a few origin stories. Sure they can be overdone—do we really need to revisit Batman's or Spider-man's origin in every single movie incarnation?—but they can also be an effective way of defining who a character is: their motivation, moral compass, and mission.

The same is true of a brand. Knowing the story behind the brand can go a long way to establishing the brand's culture. Thinking about this reminded me of a networking event I attended for small business owners and entrepreneurs.

In the space of two hours I must have heard about at least a dozen new businesses—what they did and what they were called. That's a lot of information to take in in a short time. On the drive home I did a quick mental review to see if I could recall the salient points from each conversation. I managed to recall something about everyone, but what struck me was that the first two businesses that came to mind were the two that had stories attached, and one in particular that had a story attached to the brand name.

Brand names with a story behind them stick.

Several years ago I wrote a regular marketing newsletter that included the stories and histories behind some of the most well-known brand names. That section was the most popular part of the newsletter.

It gave me the idea of maybe writing a book on the subject, but then I found out that someone had already done it. Evan Morris' fun book, *From Altoids to Zima* (Morris 2004), is now one of the most thumbed books on my marketing book shelf.

There is a story behind most company and brand names. I've worked for companies named after bags of chips, science fiction villains, a historical event, and even one that got its name from a typo.

> Discover your origin story—tell your origin story. People will remember it, and they will remember you.

Originally published on LinkedIn, November 24, 2015

26

Collaboration is the Pits, and it Can Drive Success

Hot Pit Pass — Those words on the ticket hanging around my neck on a fancy lanyard were magic to me—access to the epicenter of the action in a major motor race.

A few years ago my wife and I were invited to attend the Texas NASCAR race as a guest of Richard Childress Racing, and part of the package was a guided tour of their pit operations and the coveted pass, which allowed us to stay in the pit area for the whole race.

NASCAR is unmatched in the access it gives fans and visitors, and with that magic piece of paper we got to wander anywhere, including sitting on the pit wall watching the cars come in and be serviced.

It was a magic moment witnessing the well-rehearsed choreography of a top-flight pit crew. Six men flowed over the wall to service the car, filling it with fuel and changing four wheels and tires in less than 15 seconds.[1]

---

[1] In Formula One racing, where the pit crew can number as high as fourteen people, each with a dedicated task, they can complete a four wheel and tire change in two to three seconds!

A good pit stop can mean the difference between success and failure in a race, and a good pit crew can be just as important as the driver when it comes to positioning a car to win. Despite there only being one person on the track, motor racing is definitely a team sport.

This was brought home to me again during a business trip while watching the 2015 NASCAR race in Atlanta on the hotel room TV. Not surprisingly, I've stayed a fan of the Richard Childress Racing teams and always follow them closely, especially the Caterpillar-sponsored #31 team. During the Atlanta race the #31 pit crew were exceptional, as it soon became apparent that with every pit stop the car emerged several positions ahead of where it had entered. In some cases the fast, efficient work of the team gaining four or five places.

It strikes me that the pit-crew model is a perfect analogy for the content creation and delivery process. Customers are looking to your content to provide answers, and as the content creator you may feel like the lone driver out on track fighting for space and hoping to get out front and be noticed first.

But the truth is that most customer answers need input and information from across your organization. Customers don't think in terms of your operational silos, so they don't look for information in neatly packaged chunks. To meet your customers' needs you need to collaborate with subject-matter experts, do research, and then pull it all together in a language that your customers will understand.

You need to pull together your own pit crew around a particular subject, value their individual inputs, and work together to develop a process that delivers a result that will help you and your customer move forward at an accelerated pace.

Collaboration of this type results in a premium, consistent brand experience that ensures that customers get the same answer and the same information no matter which channel they use.

Working together results in success for both you and your customers.

Originally published on LinkedIn, May 19, 2015

27

Enter The Jargon

I occasionally use my Content Pool Twitter feed[1] to post a series of content marketing tips. Among them was the following:

> To create readable content, avoid jargon and acronyms.

It seems a logical and obvious piece of advice, and not one I'd given much additional thought to, until I was asked the question, "What do you mean by jargon?" My immediate answer was "Terms used exclusively within your industry that wouldn't be understood by people outside of it." But I've begun to question that answer.

Webster's dictionary defines jargon as *the technical terminology or characteristic idiom of a special activity or group*, which seems to fit with my original answer. But how do you define that group, and where are its boundaries?

When does jargon become acceptable?

Think about the number of technical terms that are now part of everyday conversation: download, upgrade, etc. Do they still count as computer-industry jargon?

---

[1] https://twitter.com/thecontentpool

What started me down this line of thought was doing some seasonal promotional work for my book about wikis. In conversation with friends in the technical community I tend to use the word *wiki* without a second thought. It's a word well understood in that community, and I guess it could be considered industry jargon.

A few days ago a pop-culture writer friend of mine posted on his blog that he was doing some research on "the wiki." He, of course, meant he had been using Wikipedia, which is just one (extreme) example of a wiki implementation.

His use of a generic term for the technology made me wonder: is the word wiki moving away from jargon to becoming mainstream? If it is, what does this mean for professional communicators trying to avoid jargon?

To return to my earlier question, at what point does a word move from being jargon, which should be avoided, to a generally understood term that's perfectly acceptable to use with a broader audience? Is jargon a label that is only proportional to the size of the community that accepts and understands a specific definition of a word, so that the smaller the community the more likely a word is to be labeled as jargon?

This is something you need to consider when preparing or editing content for consumption. The prime tenet of writing, "know your audience," should be applied strictly when it comes to deciding whether a term is or is not jargon. You need to know what the customer knows and make sure you communicate clearly without any underlying assumptions.

Originally published on LinkedIn, December 1, 2015

28

Ditch the FAQ: Design for a Frictionless Experience

All I wanted was some sushi.

You wouldn't believe how difficult it was to find out if any of the three sushi restaurants within walking distance of my hotel were actually open. Their websites were full of text that explained the ambiance, the chef's background, and even the history of the restaurant (and in one case the historic building that it was located in).

The pictures of neatly arranged and presented sushi rolls and specialties looked pretty and further whetted my appetite. But they still didn't answer my question nor did they help me navigate the website to find the answer to my question: is this restaurant open now?

FAQs don't make up for a poor site

I eventually found the information I wanted in the *Frequently Asked Questions* page, which got me thinking: if you still have a FAQ page, then you are implicitly acknowledging that the rest of your website is full of information that no one wants. You are ignoring the questions that will optimize the customer journey.

Why do customers come to your website, or use your mobile app, in the first place? What are they trying to achieve? I think that people engage with a restaurant website to find three things (and rarely do they need anything else):

- ► the location
- ► the operating hours
- ► the menu

So many pages, so little useful information

I once worked on a project for a large company whose website was a perfect reflection of its corporate and business unit structure. It had a lot of FAQ pages—each business unit had its own. So many that even their employees had a hard time finding information.

Our analysis showed that 80% of the website traffic was to look up product specifications, get pricing, buy spare parts, or get support. Once we rebuilt the website to make those tasks as easy as possible, traffic, leads, and online parts sales revenue increased.

Structure your digital experience around supplying the critical information your customer needs in the easiest way possible, then optimize the details through testing.

Your goal: a frictionless digital experience

Use testing to develop a frictionless experience. Test if your text and graphics help drive the experience. It doesn't matter if picture A gets more hits than picture B if neither helps drive the experience. Look at click-through rates and subsequent customer actions.

If you drive the experience using graphics, make sure they are composed and positioned to help customers. For instance, shots that guide people's eyes towards the next call to action generate more click-throughs than posed shots of models looking straight out of the page.

Test to make sure that the page layouts, paths, text, and graphics are appropriate for the market and culture. Does the experience change based on the level of the customer engagement and where they are in their journey? Do you have your customer journey mapped out and know which parts of the digital experience map to which steps in that journey?

Remember, optimizing through testing is not about A versus B—it's about removing the friction from the experience. I don't care if the Dragon Roll looks prettier than the California Roll if I can't find out when you're open for business.

Originally published on CMS Wire, October 6, 2016

29

Beer is Content ... and so is Bacon

"Beer is Content"

I saw that quote pop up on my Twitter stream one day, and it made me smile.[1] While it seemed like a cute saying, I couldn't figure out any relevant context, except maybe as a t-shirt slogan.

I got the context a few days later when a travel trip took me through Dallas Fort-Worth airport. As I was walking from the nearest Starbucks back to my gate I passed the usual line up of airport eateries including representative samples from various chains. Since it was mid-morning, most were quiet, and the various hosts and hostesses were leaning against the doors looking suitably bored.

This was true for all except the host from TGI Friday's. He had stepped out into the flow of passengers walking by and was politely trying to engage a few in conversation. As I got closer I saw him zero in on a group of about five guys in their mid-twenties.

---

[1] My apologies—I've forgotten who posted it.

"Are you guys hungry?" he asked, "Maybe in need of a cold beer?"

They stopped. He quickly engaged his potential customers by offering them a solution to their immediate need. Once he had their attention he started to talk to them about various items on the menu.

He was multichannel publishing the content he had on hand. Content that had been originally developed for print was now being used as audio. He was supplementing it by adding a few value statements and pointing out photos of particular items, adding a little graphical content to the mix.

Once he got to the bacon burger, he'd hooked his new customers, and he happily showed them inside to a waiting table.

Watching all this it struck me that in this instance the food and drink, the way they were presented, and the promise of how they could solve an immediate need were as much a part of the content marketing mix as the words on the menu.

Maybe in this case "Beer is content" ... and the bacon too.

Do you consider your products or services as part of the content mix? How is product design integrated into your content strategy (if at all)?

If you'll pardon the pun: it's all food for thought.

Originally published on LinkedIn, January 12, 2016

30

Signs an eCommerce Site Doesn't Want Your Business

I don't normally spend too much of my free time thinking about my friend's cycling shorts. In fact, I can honestly say I'd given the subject zero attention until recently. My friend Don and I were at an industry forum event, and on a coffee break our conversation turned to ordering things online.

A lost sale in the making

Don mentioned he was growing frustrated with a well-known online retailer because he was finding it almost impossible to replace his favorite brand of cycling shorts. Don knew exactly what brand and style of shorts he wanted but was undecided on the color. He knew the site he wanted to buy them from stocked the right shorts, but he just couldn't find them.

The faceted search was no help—it didn't include cycling shorts as a category. The general search gave too many results, and he didn't want to wade through all of them. He knew exactly what he wanted and felt he should be able to get to it with one or two clicks at the most. He also expected that when he did get to the right page it would show a series of images so he could compare colors.

We all share this set of expectations these days.

You think of something you need, do a quick search, find the item, look at the images to confirm it's the right item, make sure the price is right, click, and order. When it works it feels close to magic. But it only needs one mismatch of data, a missing image, or a poor search strategy to derail the experience.

A picture is worth …

Having the correct image of a product has become essential to delivering a good customer experience. Customers often use images as they decide whether to make a purchase. Having clear, well-defined images with the correct data makes that decision easier for the buyer and reduces costs for the seller. It's no good getting the images right if the basic product information is missing.

Even if Don had been able to find the right color shorts, he still needed to know availability in his size, expected shipping time and delivery dates, and the price.

And pricing needs to be fed into the customer experience in a way that makes sense to the customer. Too many eCommerce sites don't display price until the last step in the process, even though the price is often the first thing a prospective customer wants to know.

A happy ending for the competition

Delivering a solid eCommerce customer experience is a combination of good digital asset management, product information management, search-engine optimization, localization, and customer insights.

And for those of you who are wondering, Don got his shorts from another seller.

Originally published on CMS Wire, May 5, 2017

31

Avoid Brand Disasters with a Visual Content Strategy

A flawed hero

I was leading the marketing content delivery group at a major equipment manufacturer, and we'd just posted a new "hero" shot on our website. We were very proud of the image: a burly, rugged-looking guy on a job site standing in front of one our machines. A perfect illustration of our brand.

Or so we thought, until I logged into email the next morning to find my inbox stuffed with requests to take the image down.

Most of those requests came from one geographical market. We hadn't realized that the burly man had his shirt sleeves rolled up, and in one of our biggest, most important, markets that was a safety violation. And safety violations were definitely not something we wanted to be seen promoting or have associated with our brand.

We quickly took down the image and added metadata that it wasn't to be used in certain markets. On reflection, we should have done this first. But like many large companies, we drew content from across the enterprise as well as from outside suppliers and agencies.

Customers don't care about your silos

The man in the shirt sleeves got us thinking: did different parts of the company use different images to represent the same things based on their local and business knowledge? Did they assume an implied level of knowledge about the subject and its applicability? Do the images just reflect the silo-ed make-up of the business's structure? How was metadata applied—if at all—to ensure correct usage and attribution?

Most importantly: how did all this affect the customer's experience when interacting with our brand across different channels around the globe?

It doesn't matter how your company is organized or what separate lines of business you have. As far as your customer is concerned every interaction with you is a representation of your brand, and they expect a consistent experience. But it must also be a consistent experience that is relevant to them and their locale.

Creating a visual content strategy

So how do you deliver a consistent brand representation while still being aware of localization and cultural issues? Our answer was to develop a visual content strategy by asking ourselves the following series of questions:

- ► What do we want our images to do? Showcase our products? Showcase our customers? Show customers using our products?

- ► What business need do we want our images to help achieve? Engage prospects and lead to click-through and lead capture? Educate and help customers with self-service, thereby reducing support costs?

► What types of images should we use to reflect our brand? Photographic and realistic or inspirational and abstract?

► Where will the images be used? Global generic images? Regional and local application? If regional, how localized?

Next, we looked at the images that we were already delivering or had in development. Did they match the business drivers outlined in our visual content strategy? If not, we stopped using them.

Content for the sake of content, no matter how pretty it looks, is a waste of resources and opportunity.

Take a detailed look at how your products are represented and localized. After the shirt-sleeves incident, we decided that the main product shot for the equipment product pages on our website would be just the machine against a plain white background.

Presenting the equipment in a consistent way made it stand out and avoided localization issues. The job-site shots were relegated to a gallery that could be customized based on the customer's location.

The next step was to develop a strong metadata model, which we applied to the images to ensure that we used the same images to show the same ideas and concepts. We attached data that fit our workflow and allowed us to deliver a customer experience that reinforced our brand. That required us to balance consistency with creativity.

Delivering consistent experiences

Once the strategy and metadata architecture was in place, we reinforced the need to store and manage images so that they could be easily located and used in the correct manner.

Our *Digital Asset Management (DAM)* system was key to delivering a consistent visual user experience. I'd recommend starting with an achievable objective, such as using a DAM to drive your website, and then growing it organically across the enterprise to cover other delivery channels. If you get people used to using it and prove that it provides value, it will lead to an improved customer experience.

In case you were wondering, the incident with the man in the short sleeves, and the subsequent development of the visual content strategy, helped my team develop and deliver a DAM-based platform that quickly grew to an enterprise solution with over one million assets that could be tracked and reused to send the correct message in the correct market.

Originally published on CMS Wire, September 1, 2016

32

DAMs Spread Across the Enterprise

Digital Asset Management (DAM) systems can benefit anyone who needs to distribute, use, and control brand-approved images. So it seems only natural that DAM systems should reside in the marketing department.

Yet while they may start there, the uses of both the assets and the DAM's functionality quickly stretch everywhere across a company.

DAM casts a wide net

When I ran the content management team at a manufacturing company, the DAM platform was originally introduced to control the flow of approved images to the company's online presence. We were revamping the website and eCommerce platform. A key part of the project was to improve the images used and to make sure they were both brand and safety compliant.

It quickly became apparent that the process involved not just storing the images but also developing a visual content strategy. Before too long, the word spread that we now had a single, safe source for brand-approved images.

The next logical step was to ensure that our print publications—such as sales brochures, technical specifications, and marketing collateral—all pulled images from the same source.

Soon we were talking to other groups in the company, and even our dealer network, about how they could contribute to and access the DAM. Instead of just storing the images selected for use on the website, we were storing every picture from any product photo shoot.

Suddenly the company archives became interesting to a wider range of people. In the space of 18 months we had passed one million assets with over 8,000 users accessing them.

Unexpected DAM use cases

The most interesting result was how the DAM became the source for applications and use cases we had never considered. We had developed a way to create lightweight 3-D models of our products and had started storing the source files for those on the DAM, too. The DAM became the source driving augmented-reality proof-of-concept innovations. It also was used to populate digital signage at dealer showrooms as well as images for training, facilities planning, trade shows, coffee-table art books, calendars, licensed merchandise, and more.

By the time I left the company, we had recorded sixteen different use cases across the company for the content stored in the DAM, and I'm sure there are even more now.

From aerospace to HR

The thing is, I was far from alone in witnessing how a company can use a good DAM platform in different, powerful ways. I've seen other other organizations take advantage of DAMs, including:

> ► Media companies that use their DAM to deliver DVD packaging and advertising banners for different markets and distribution channels, automatically resizing images and placing logos and text that match the intended use.

- ► Drink companies that make the DAM a central component of their high-profile sports sponsorship programs.

- ► A rail company that uses the DAM to manage rail inspection videos from cameras mounted on the front of locomotives.

- ► An aerospace engine company that uses its DAM to store and analyze images of parts from any engine involved in an accident.

- ► A museum that created a DAM-driven production line to scan thousands of physical objects from their collections and put them online, giving access to information on historical objects that are rarely seen.

- ► Legal and HR departments that use search functions and DAM metadata to build reports that show when certain people appear in images or when and where particular tag lines are used.

Once you have a fully functional digital asset management system with a usable set of assets combined with a well-defined metadata schema and a visual content strategy, you'll turn to it as your single, safe source for enterprise imagery, videos, and more.

Originally published on CMS Wire, August 15, 2017

33

That Emotional Warning Light

I've long been an advocate of the advantages of using a controlled authoring vocabulary in producing technical content. The concept of one word = one meaning is central to this concept and underpins standards such as Simplified Technical English (STE).

Clearly, ambiguity can lead to mistakes and, in extreme cases, can even cause fatalities. But one thing I hadn't thought about before is that in addition to considering the literal meanings of the words and phrases used, we should also consider the emotional and psychological impact.

It was an article by veteran racer and motoring journalist Denise McCluggage that opened my eyes on this subject. Denise's article discussed the impact of the Check Engine warning light common in most vehicles today. By all the rules and principles of controlled authoring, the typical warning light is perfectly valid. It is clear, concise, and uses simple words and symbols with well-defined meanings.

But as Denise points out, it has the potential for two distinctly different emotional impacts.

For a typical car enthusiast (like me), the response to the Check Engine warning may be "Rats, I need to take my car to the dealer at some point, where they will do some minor adjustment and charge me an arm and a leg." After a while, when the car doesn't do anything untoward, I may even ignore the warning altogether.

But for some other drivers, the Check Engine light raises an immediate concern that the engine, the very thing that makes the car go, is about to fail and leave them stranded at the side of the road or even cause a life-threatening situation.

So what does Check Engine actually mean? In most cases it is an indication that "something might be amiss with the emission system and you should really have it looked at next time you are in the shop for routine maintenance."

So the choice of words is not as good as I first thought it was. Maybe it should read "Emission Controls Service Due."

In short, the article made me realize that in addition to using the right vocabulary, we need to pay attention to context and audience psychology.

Preparing customer-facing content, be it for marketing, operations, or service, is not just about passing on knowledge, it's also about the context where your content is seen and the emotion with which the message is received.

Originally published on LinkedIn, September 29, 2015

34

Your CX Testing Isn't Done 'til it Passes the "Buddy Bob" Test

"Do you think our customers will like the image of the kitten better than the one of the puppy?"

If you think digital experience testing comes down to resolving questions like this, you are missing the bigger picture.

Testing means more than click throughs

Test to make sure that your content—text, graphics, video, audio—helps drive the overall experience. It doesn't matter if the kitten gets more hits than the puppy if neither helps your customers get the information they need. Look at click-through rates and subsequent customer actions.

Check to make sure your graphics are composed and positioned to help customers on their journey. For instance, shots that guide people's eyes in the direction of the next call to action generate far more click-throughs than thoughtfully posed shots of smiling models looking straight out of the page.

Refining the digital experience focuses on the user interface as well as content design, but you also need to make sure you understand how they work together.

Test to make sure the page layouts, paths, text, and graphics are market and culture appropriate. Does the experience change based on the level of the customer engagement and where they are in their journey? Is the logged-in experience more personalized than the guest experience? It should be.

Do you have your customer journey mapped out and know which parts of the digital experience map to which steps in that journey?

How about the language you use? Is your website, mobile app, digital signage, augmented-reality solution, or whatever you use to deliver your digital experience littered with jargon, acronyms, and industry terms that you and your team understand but which are meaningless to customers?

Names are important. Think about what you call something. Don't expect the customer to know the terms you use internally. Pick names that the customer will recognize and use them consistently.

Don't take it from the insiders

Once you've done your final internal testing and maybe even met with a focus group or two, I suggest you employ the final and best test: the "Buddy Bob" test. Ask your family and friends to walk through your planned experience design.

Make sure whoever does the testing has no knowledge of your industry, your company processes, etc. The more removed they are from your role in designing, testing, and delivering digital experiences, the better. Ask them to do a task a new customer would want to do, such as create an account and find some basic information.

It's amazing how often we leave out basic information as we design online interactions. Once we become familiar with a particular environment, especially one we created ourselves, we have an almost intuitive baseline of knowledge—knowledge someone outside of the community does not have. Answering "it's obvious" to any question raised during testing is not acceptable.

If Bob and your other friends repeatedly ask the same questions about a part of your process, that part is broken and you need to fix it. And not in a way that makes it easier for you, but in a way that it makes it easier for the customer to complete their task.

Remember, it doesn't matter which picture gets more clicks if I can't find basic information, such as how your products can help me, how to buy them, where you do business, or how I can talk with someone to learn more.

Originally published on CMS Wire, April 6, 2017

35

Beware the Content Fallacy

In recent months I've seen a lot of people posting and re-posting an interesting infographic[1] that showcases the "30 Technologies of the Next Decade." It's an impressive list of where digital transformation is taking us and how the customer experience will change in the relatively near term.

One thing that's clear: our technology stack is going through a period of dramatic change.

Over the last year or so I've also been privy to the plans of some major organizations across a wide range of industries. These plans map out their aspirational goals for addressing the challenges such change will bring. I've seen a lot of systems and architecture diagrams, proofs of concept, and prototypes demonstrated with varying degrees of success. And, with a few exceptions, they all share a common weakness.

I estimate that at least half of those 30 technologies depend on content—be it written, graphical, video, audio, animation, or developing media like augmented reality—to deliver the customer experience.

---

[1]"The Top 30 Emerging Technologies (2018–2028)" (Moffitt 2018).

Yet many of those future-looking plans that embrace those technologies suffer from what I term "The Content Fallacy." That is, an unstated belief that "content just happens."

Content needs to be engineered

A common trope when talking about the impact of digital transformation is to focus on the end result. This is good; we all need a shared vision. However, the road to achieving that vision too often omits a critical piece: *content engineering*.

To achieve any sort of personalized, high-quality experience across a growing number of delivery channels, you need to think up front as to what sort of content you will need and how it will be engineered to achieve those goals.

To give you a real-world example, when discussing with a client how to meet a C-suite-level mandate for personalizing the customer experience as part of their digital transformation strategy, we discovered that to meet all the different vectors of marketing campaigns, product types, customer segments, industries, languages, and delivery channels they were targeting, they would be potentially delivering over 18,000 variants of one piece of content.

They assumed that because they already had the baseline content, they could just feed that content into their new systems, and it would be delivered in the format the customer needed. However, content for a website is not the same content you need for a smart phone or watch. The content you have was most likely not written or structured for the question-context-interpretation-answer model you need for a chatbot or voice assistant.

If your customer communications have primarily been text-based, then they probably will not work alongside visuals or provide the right context and enhancement for an augmented-reality experience.

The six facets of content engineering

Content engineering is a six-faceted approach to thinking and designing your content for the emerging digital transformation experience. The team at [A], the content intelligence service company, defines those facets as follows:[2]

- ► **Model:** a representation of the types of content you create, including their elements, attributes, and relationships.

- ► **Metadata:** information that helps applications, authors, systems, and robots use content in a smart way.

- ► **Mark-up:** a way to identify the structure and context of the content outside the content itself.

- ► **Schema:** a form of metadata that provides meaning and relationships to content. Schemas are often published as standard vocabularies. Examples of XML schemas include DocBook, DITA, and TEI.

- ► **Taxonomy:** a map of related concepts which are applied to content, often as tags. They enable and support features such as related-content reuse, navigation, search, and personalization.

- ► **Topology:** the art of developing common organizational structures and containers across content management and publishing systems.

By taking an engineering approach, content moves away from being something that just happens (and then often doesn't deliver the expected results) to becoming the foundational fuel to power digital transformation and deliver those exciting new multi-channel experiences we are all looking forward to.

Originally published on CMS Wire, October 2, 2018

---

[2]"What Is Content Engineering?" ([A] 2016)

36

AI's Missing Ingredient: Intelligent Content

My Saturday mornings used to be full of *artificial intelligence* (AI). Thanks to the TV shows I watched and the comics and books I read, I grew up expecting to live in a world of robots that could think and talk, vehicles that would whisk me off to far-away destinations with no need for drivers or pilots, and computers that would respond to voice commands and know the answer to just about everything.

I may not yet have that robot butler, and my first experience with a self-driving car left me more apprehensive than impressed, but in other ways artificial intelligence is now part of my everyday existence, and in ways that I don't even think about.

One of the first things I do each morning is ask Siri for the day's weather forecast and then check to make sure that my Nest thermostat is reacting accordingly. During the day, Pandora's predictive analytics choose my music, and in the evening Netflix serves up my favorite shows and movies. My books arrive courtesy of Amazon, and there's a fair chance that some of those purchases were driven by recommendations generated via AI.

Outdated practices hamper AI advances

This is all great stuff, but it's just a small representation of the promise of AI, and that promise has not yet been realized.

Many companies and organizations still use older technology and systems that get in the way of a truly seamless AI customer experience. As long as companies build systems that don't interact, build point-solution silos, duplicate processes across business units, or fail to take a holistic view of their content assets, AI systems will continue to pull from a restricted set of information.

Over the past few years, as I have talked and worked with companies that are pursuing AI initiatives, I have noticed that the majority of those projects fail for a common reason; AI needs *intelligent content*. It may not be the only reason, but it's a common denominator.

AI needs intelligent content

No artificial intelligence proof of concept, pilot program, or full implementation will scale without the fuel that connects systems to users—content. And not just any content, but the right content at the right time to answer a question or move through a process.

AI can help automate mundane tasks and free up humans to be more creative, but it needs the underpinning of data in context: specifically, content that is intelligent. According to Ann Rockley and Charles Cooper, intelligent content is "content that's structurally rich and semantically categorized and therefore automatically discoverable, reusable, reconfigurable, and adaptable."[1]

The way we deliver and interact with content is changing. It used to be good enough to create large monolithic pieces of content: manuals, white papers, print brochures, etc. and publish them in either a traditional broadcast model or a passive mode. We would then hope that, in the best case, we could drive our customers to find our content or, in the worst case, that whoever needed it would stumble across it via search or navigation.

---

[1] *Managing Enterprise Content* (Rockley 2012)

With the rise of new delivery channels and AI-driven algorithms, that has changed. We no longer want to just consume content, we want to have conversations with it. The broadcast model has changed to an invoke-and-respond model. To meet the needs of the new delivery models like AI, our content needs to be active and to be delivered proactively.

We need to build intelligent content that supports advanced publishing processes that leverage data and metadata, coordinate content efforts across departmental silos, and make smart use of technology, including, increasingly, artificial intelligence and machine learning.

In addition to Rockley and Cooper's definition of intelligent content, our content should also be modular, coherent, self-aware, and quantum. Here are definitions of those four characteristics:

- ► **Modular:** existing in smaller, self-contained units of information that address single topics.

- ► **Coherent:** defined, described, and managed through a common content model so that it can be moved across systems.

- ► **Self-Aware:** connected with semantics, taxonomy, structure, and context.

- ► **Quantum:** made up of content segments that can exist in multiple states and systems at the same time.

Intelligent content with a common content and semantics model that allows systems to talk the same language when moving content across silos may be the key to unlocking the technology disconnect that is holding AI back from even greater acceptance.[2]

Originally published on CMS Wire, April 4, 2018

---

[2]For more on intelligent content, a good starting place is Ann Rockley, Charles Cooper, and Scott Abel's book *Intelligent Content* (Rockley 2015).

Context

context (*noun*)
con·text /ˈkäntekst/

- ► The circumstances that form the setting for an event, statement, or idea and help it be fully understood and assessed.
- ► The parts of something written or spoken that immediately precede and follow a word or passage and clarify its meaning.
- ► **Similar:** circumstances, conditions, surroundings, factors, situation, environment, background, mood, frame of reference.

37

Should Customers Pay for the Manual?

Not long ago the following popped up on a friend's Twitter feed:

OMG! (Company Name) actually charges for their owner's manuals! That's absurd.

Absurd? Really? Is that the common expectation—that all the manuals associated with a product should be free?

At various points over the years, I worked with two companies that had almost identical competing product lines. Each had around 50% of the market (although actual market leadership tended to fluctuate between them on a year-to-year basis), yet they had diametrically opposed philosophies when it came to supplying documentation.

Company A had the philosophy that when you buy their product you get everything needed to run, maintain, and operate it (but not to repair it), so they included the cost of producing the documentation in their product pricing. They made their money on spare parts.

Company B had the philosophy that when you buy their product, you just buy the product and everything else is extra to be purchased as needed, so they had a lower product price and charged for their documentation (and spare parts, too).

The total cost of ownership for both products over the normal operating span turned out to be just about the same.

Let's take a look at the two scenarios in more detail.

Company A: documentation included

This is the more traditional model. A content development team writes manuals, help sets, etc. and publishes a complete suite of documentation, which is delivered with the product. That suite can range from one small manual to (in the case of an aircraft) hundreds of large volumes. The cost of producing those manuals is covered in the product cost, and the customer perceives them as being free.

When the cost is accounted for, this approach works well. However, I'm amazed at the number of times I've done consulting work for companies that don't even consider the cost of the documentation. They don't calculate it, they don't consider it a development cost, and they don't cover it in the price of their products.

Often companies like that consider documentation to be a necessary evil (a phrase I have heard more than once) and an uncontrolled overhead. As a result, content development is not considered an integral part of the design and production process and is poorly funded (if at all). The result is usually poor quality documentation.

As a general rule of thumb, if you buy a low-priced commodity product that includes everything, there is a fair chance that the manuals will be next to useless. (I know this is a broad stroke statement, and there are always exceptions, but it is too often true.)

However, when managed well, this scenario has the often overlooked advantage that it breaks down internal silos. Because the cost of the content is already covered, content becomes an enterprise asset instead of being pinned to one department's revenue stream.

In addition, more and more companies have discovered that giving customers early and free access to operation information reduces sales cycles and cost, making technical content the unsung hero of content marketing. By the time customers engage with the sales team, most of their questions have been answered, and they are better informed and ready to engage.

Covering the cost of documentation centrally and delivering it with the product also makes it easier to innovate around content and roll out new delivery platforms and technologies, such as augmented reality. It also allows you to combine documentation with other content such as training, marketing materials, or eCommerce platforms to deliver an integrated customer experience.

Company B: documentation sold separately

In this model, the cost of producing and distributing the product documentation is usually well understood and managed. Most products using this model include a small documentation set that shows customers how to get started and perform simple operations with the expectation that if customers want to know more they will be prepared to spend money.

The manual in your car's glove compartment is a good example. It covers driver operations, but people who want to maintain and repair their car will go and buy a book on how to do it. There are whole companies that write and sell specialist manuals for car dealers and repair shops. The vast majority of customers will never access a full documentation suite, so why provide it to everyone? The manufacturer can focus on producing the documentation that 80% of its customers need, and the other 20% can be covered by add-on, specialist manuals that provide a recognizable revenue stream.

One area of opportunity where the pay-as-you-need-it model breaks down is that currently most manuals you pay for (including the one that my friend was complaining about) are PDFs of traditional print manuals. You still end up buying the complete book even if you only want one or two sections. If you have a pay-to-download-the-manual model, why not publish it based on topics or specific tasks and use a system of micro-payments? Instead of asking customers to pay $10 (the amount that outraged my friend), $15, or $20 for the whole manual, why not charge $0.99 per topic?

If you go the separate-charge route, it gives the customer a choice, lowers product prices, and transforms the content development team from being overhead into a profit center.

On a personal note, when I switched one documentation department from being an overhead to being a revenue generator it completely changed the way the role of documentation, and the people who produced it, was perceived.

So which one is the right approach? I think they both are. Whether or not you charge for documentation is a product of factors such as the business plan, the content development team's role in your organization, customer expectations, etc.

However, one underlying principle that applies in either case is that the cost of documentation development should be correctly calculated and factored into the product development costs. You need to recoup that cost somewhere; you just need to decide where to include the cost in the product life cycle and how to account for it.

Originally published on LinkedIn, November 3, 2015

38

Let the Customer Experience Drive Your Technology Design

It all started with a new Christmas decoration my wife had set her heart on. She'd been back and forth wondering if she should buy it. After a lot of discussion, we found ourselves back in the store, where she decided it would be ideal for a space on the hallway table.

And so we found ourselves at the register, ready to pay for the new decoration. As is the case at most stores these days, the transaction was processed through a payment-terminal card reader. You know, the sort where you can either insert or slide your card or sometimes even wave your phone over it to pay for goods. It was no different from the hundreds of other terminals that we have encountered when shopping. In addition to the places where you could insert your card, it had a screen, a keypad, and an electronic touch pen.

All went well until my wife got to a screen asking her to confirm the amount. The green OK icon on the screen was an exact image of the green OK button on the keypad, so she pressed the button on the keypad. Several times. Nothing happened. I tried it too. Still nothing. At which point the sales associate smiled and said, "Oh, everyone does that. You need to press OK on the touchscreen."

An experience problem

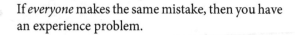

If *everyone* makes the same mistake, then you have an experience problem.

There was no text or other indication that the OK icon was active or that the OK button was inactive. So why was the OK icon made to look exactly like the corresponding button on the keypad? Or why wasn't the system designed to accept input from either the screen or the keypad?

Two steps later, after my wife had inserted her debit card, the screen flashed up a question asking what sort of card it was. Why didn't it recognize the card from the data swipe? And the list of options it gave for the card type were clearly being driven from a back-end financial system; the option names had no relevance to the average shopper. The sales associate had a cheat-sheet that allowed her to identify the correct response needed for the average bank-issued debit card.

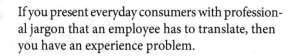

If you present everyday consumers with professional jargon that an employee has to translate, then you have an experience problem.

Focus on the needs of the user

Our shopping trip got me thinking about customer experience technology. It used to be that most technology interfaces with a customer interaction point were system-specific: one type of action was served and captured by one piece of technology. However, as the customer-experience technology stack has evolved, we now have single interaction points that are either driven by, or feed, multiple back-end systems. We also have, as was the case with the payment terminal, interfaces that combine different ways of entering responses or acknowledging actions.

Deciding when to use which action and which technology to use can be a difficult trade-off, but too often those decisions are driven by the limitations of the technology rather than the needs of the user. By the time my wife had finished paying for her decoration, she had used the screen, the keypad, and the pen. Why did that transaction need three separate types of action when it all could have been done on a touchscreen?

Experience should inform design

I've long been a believer that system limitations shouldn't drive the experience. Rather, the experience should inform the system's design. As the technology stack continues to evolve, we shouldn't be throwing new technologies at individual problems, we should be taking a holistic, outside-in view of how those new solutions will affect the way our customers do business with us and building our customer-facing systems based on that holistic view.

Originally published on CMS Wire, December 12, 2017

39

Why Your Customer Data Platform Is a Failure

"Account number, please." Three simple words tell me I am about to have a less than optimal customer experience.

It's an all too familiar scenario: I call up a company, and the phone system asks me to punch in my account number to verify who I am. And then every time I get passed on to another step in the process, I am asked again to give my account number and verify my name.

Derailed by data silos

It's an obvious tell that the company I'm calling has its customer data silo-ed in systems that don't talk to each other. Once I punch my account number into a supposedly automated system, that data, and the customer profile associated with it, should travel with me on every subsequent interaction, no matter who is handling my call at the moment or which department that person works in.

Isn't that the promise that customer data platforms (CDP) are supposed to deliver? After all, CDP technology is designed to provide a persistent, unified customer database to other systems across the enterprise. But is that really what's happening? Too often, companies see CDPs solely as marketing tools and, as a consequence, keep them silo-ed within specific marketing-driven operational functions. These companies use CDPs to drive marketing campaigns, not to improve the customer experience.

Look at your company the way customers do

When marketers talk about the omnichannel experience, they are usually referring to the various channels through which they deliver their messages: websites, social media, email, etc. It's an inside-out viewpoint built around a broadcast model. They are failing to look at their company the way their customers do—as a single entity.

When customers engage with you, they don't do so because they are anxious to consume your latest marketing message, they do so because they want a question answered. They don't want to passively consume, they want to engage in some sort of conversational relationship that will provide value and help them.

More to the point, they don't care which functional group or department the information they need comes from. They don't know your business-unit structure or your operational hierarchy. To them, your company is a single entity, and every interaction with that entity is a reflection of your brand experience.

Asking a customer to supply the same information again and again is a bad brand experience.

If your CDP acts solely as a silo-ed enabler of marketing campaigns and doesn't improve the customer experience, then it is failing.

Originally published on CMS Wire, July 11, 2018

40

Don't Dismantle Data Silos, Build Bridges

I used to be a strident proponent of breaking down system silos. Over the years, I took the stage at conferences and preached that tearing down walls between various pieces of technology across the organization would help deliver a better customer experience. But not any longer. I now realize that this is an impossible dream.

Let's face it: no one is going to throw out their incumbent systems just because you say they should. Especially not if those systems still do the job they were purchased to do.

We have all worked with systems that are good enough to fulfill a specific set of tasks. Replacing such a system isn't quick or cheap, but the biggest hurdle isn't budget or technology (although that's what's often cited)—it's human.

Navigating the shifting CX waters

People often build their careers around particular systems. They develop specific areas of knowledge related to *their* system and *their* data. The idea of letting others into their area of expertise is threatening. It's a world of what ifs. What if they (the other departments) mess up my data? What if their findings contradict mine?

Then there's the cultural aspect. Systems become ingrained to the point that policies and procedures develop around them, and they become an essential part of the way the company operates. It may not be the best way, and often it isn't, but if it works why change it?

> Change is hard, and dramatic change is the hardest of all. But change is inevitable.

The way customers interact with companies is evolving and so are their expectations. It has always taken a combination of divisions and departments to deliver goods, services, and the desired brand experience to customers. Similarly, customers have always interacted with organizations via multiple touchpoints spread across multiple departments. Those differences in customer experience were once an accepted part of doing business, but they no longer are.

Today's customers demand a seamless, consistent experience at every interaction with the company, both before and after purchase. Delivering a series of disparate transactions will no longer cut it. Organizations must develop ongoing relationships, and to do that, they need to take a holistic view of the customer's data—data that resides in those silo-ed systems.

Build bridges between systems of record

Watching two characters from Game of Thrones negotiate across a castle drawbridge, instead of just battling things out, got me thinking about information flow. Instead of tearing down the castle (or system) walls, look at how you can build bridges between systems. That way those who have built a body of expertise can share it while still having authority over their own keep (data set).

Bridges allow data to be collected once and then flow freely between systems, allowing individual system owners to use that data in a way that suits their needs. Each customer-interfacing system can still stand alone and address the needs of a particular line of business or the enterprise as a whole. But by allowing data to pass between systems, including internal enterprise systems, your company can create a connected, continuous customer experience.

Over a period of time you will find out which systems you really need and which data is central to delivering the customer experience. Some silos will gradually fall into disuse and fade away to be replaced by true systems of record.

This was brought home to me recently when a VP at a large company told the story of their digital transformation project. Midway through the project, they realized that of the 30-plus systems they had in use, only nine were vital to the process of delivering customer service. Taking a customer-centric view of their data and the way it flowed around the organization helped them understand which were the real systems of value.

Building bridges between systems allows you to develop data journeys that reflect your customers' journeys.

Originally published on CMS Wire, January 11, 2018

41

Do I Really Need 61 Apps on My Work Phone?

Sixty-one: that was the number of apps on my company-issued cellphone at one point. These covered everything from pre-loaded, general-use apps to specialist apps for specific company needs (e.g. file sharing, product catalogs, etc.) to travel apps to conference apps to social media platforms. That's a lot of information sources.

Add in the ninety-nine apps on my personal phone, and I was carrying around a veritable smorgasbord of data in my pocket. But is it all really necessary? Of course it isn't.

So why do I feel the need to have so much data at hand? Has the abundance and ease of information we are subjected to each day reset our expectations?

So many apps, so little time

According to my phone's weekly screen use report I now spend between four and five hours a day interacting with mobile devices and apps, and from what I've read in various articles that seems to be around the normal usage pattern. And as the line between work hours and personal time continues to blur, it's hard to classify apps as either work or personal; they are spread across a continuous spectrum. Looking at the figures, I spend about 50% of that time on social media apps, about 18% on work-related, productivity apps and utilities, and around 5% on eCommerce.

So if only 20% to 25% of my mobile time is spent on work-related activities, why do I have so many work apps on my phone? The answer is "just in case."

The ease of access to information has overtaken the value of the information itself as the main driver of what we keep. Of those sixty-one apps I had on my company phone, I probably used seven of them on a daily basis, a couple of others weekly, and another ten when I traveled. Aside from the standard system-delivered apps, the rest—about 50% of the total—fell firmly into the "just in case" category.

Do I really need the conference apps for past conferences? But what happens if someone asks me about a session from that conference? With the app I can find the information in just a few clicks. Sure, I could probably find the same information online, but an app seems so much more convenient, even if it actually takes more clicks than using a search engine. It's that perception of having information at your fingertips that makes them so compelling.

Sometimes the experience becomes too much. When I get to the point that I know I have an app for a specific task but find myself swiping back and forth across multiple screens to find it, it's time to do a clean-up. If an app hasn't been used for over six months, I delete it. Unfortunately, I often find some of these same apps creep back onto my phone over the next few weeks "just in case."

How to sort through the noise?

While I may not be the best at deleting redundant or unused apps, I do manage notifications. It seems as if every app I download asks if it can send me updates and notifications. While these can be useful at times, more often than not they are a nuisance. When messages inundate my phone screen, I tend to delete then unread.

The possibility of missing something important in the noise increases with every new app I download. So I now take a much more proactive stance and rarely give notification permission. When I do it for an event-based app—since it's a useful way of keeping up with schedule and location changes—I turn off permission as soon as the event is over. And if the same app, such as a weather app, appears on both my company and personal phone, I only allow notifications on one device. That's one way to keep the number of buzzes down and make sure the important stuff gets noticed.

Really, that's the root problem with information overload—be it from mobile apps, news feeds, social media or too much email—how do we sort through the noise?

We have to decide what's important so we can balance our need to stay informed with our need to get our job done. How we manage the apps on our mobile devices is a good way to build that discipline.

But companies can also help. Corporate IT groups can step in and occasionally purge company-issued cell phones of any apps that are well past their sell-by date. Despite what I said above, I probably don't really need the apps for our last two annual conferences and the international user-group tour that took place six months ago.

It might also be useful if the companies that develop apps built in some sort of self-destruct mechanism. For example, an event-based app could delete itself at a set time after the event. Or if an app goes unused for a specific amount of time (e.g., six months or a year), it could send a notification saying the app will delete unless reactivated.

At the end of the day, we need to keep asking ourselves: is "just in case" a sufficient justification for app overload?

Originally published on CMS Wire, November 10, 2017

42

The Connected Customer Experience: Beyond the Browser

In 10 years, websites will no longer exist—at least not in the traditional sense.

Websites have been around for over twenty years, and while the presentation layers have become slicker, the vast majority are still just basically digitized brochures. But in the last few years, customer expectations have changed the way we interact in the digital world.

Customer experience on the go

Being online no longer means sitting in front of a computer screen. We can no longer assume people will be at a desk so we can drive them to websites designed to be displayed on a large screen.

Prospects and customers instead demand that we give them the information they need no matter where they are or what device they are using. And that information can't be just us trying to sell them on how great we are; it should provide them with real value by moving them along their journey as smoothly and easily as possible.

The interface to the web became the search bar, and we focused on search-engine optimization to deliver our content. Now, social media and smart phones has moved us away from interacting on desktop screens to a mobile world where interaction is the domain of the specialized app.

Along with that came an increased demand for more snackable chunks of content.

I'm not talking about the future

So what's next? Reaching customers in new ways means embracing that ever-evolving digital world.

In fact it may not be a truly digital world anymore, but rather a seamless integration of the digital and physical. Customer experience is becoming a connected experience across the *Internet of Things* (IoT). When you think about the Internet of Things and technologies such as *virtual reality* grabbing the headlines, you might relax, thinking that these technologies are years away (and some may never gain widespread adoption). However, the connected experience is already here, and we need to be delivering it.

The increasing functionality, accuracy, and integration of voice-driven digital assistants such as Siri and Alexa enable customer experiences where the complete interaction is voice driven.

Do you have an audio content strategy in place?

I'm talking here and now

While shopping at the mall I took some time to study the digital signage that is taking over from the old static maps and poster advertising. With video, touch screens, and links to the web, these signs are moving information gathering from a passive to an interactive customer experience. Add iBeacon, which broadcasts a code to the sign that uniquely identifies you, and it's a short step to delivering a totally personalized experience.

Amazon has developed and introduced a new retail experience where the store recognizes your phone as you enter, tracks what you pick up from the shelf, and charges you on the way out.

How about a store linked with an eCommerce site? Or one that tells you where to find the things you are most likely to want based on your purchase history?

If you've seen the movie *Minority Report,* this may all seem a bit familiar. But it isn't science fiction anymore. On the way home from the mall I enjoyed the drive in my car with its heads-up display and centralized screen for navigation and entertainment. That screen also displays relevant parts of the owner's manual in response to any warning light that goes off, and if I want, it will also deliver interactive, real-time driving tips.

How many other in-situ screens do we interact with on a daily basis now? Seat-back screens on a flight, ATMs, and even TV screens on gas pumps are examples of new channels for a connected customer experience.

Thinking that customer experience is all about your online presence and your call center is not enough anymore. You need to deliver just the right amount of intelligent, structured content in context, giving customers the information they need at the time they need it for the platform/location they are on.

Originally published on CMS Wire, January 4, 2017

43

So What Exactly is Omnichannel?

An angry man with a delivery van redefined my understanding of omnichannel customer experience.

Traditionally when I've referred to *omnichannel* delivery I've tended to think primarily in terms of content; it's all about making sure that we deliver the right content or messaging across multiple digital platforms such as a website, tablet, or phone. Is it a consistent experience suitably tailored for each different device?

These days when I talk about delivering an omnichannel customer experience, I include physical contact points through printed media, store-front, or call-center interaction.

What do I actually mean by omnichannel?

Let's look at some formal definitions.

The Oxford English Dictionary defines omnichannel as "denoting or relating to a type of retail that integrates the different methods of shopping available to consumers (e.g., online, in a physical store, or by phone)."

Wikipedia broadens the scope to "a cross-channel business model that companies use to increase customer experience," which seems to fit in with what I've been discussing above.

But, let's take a deeper look at the entomology, "omni" comes from the Latin word *omnis* which can mean all or universal. If you say you are delivering an omnichannel experience are you really managing and delivering a good customer experience across *every* channel that a customer can possibly use to interact with you? What about those channels outside your direct control—such as resellers, dealers, retail stores, and other third parties—that sell, implement, or support your product, adding to the overall experience?

And it's a two-way process. You might be using every channel you can think of to communicate with your customers, but are you aware of every channel that they are using to communicate with you? Over the years, when I've wanted to communicate both good and bad experiences to companies, I've written letters, phoned them, sent email, and these days I'm more than likely to post something on Twitter. Many companies monitor these obvious channels of communication, but are they catching everything?

Which brings me back to the angry man with the van. He was so unhappy with his van that he painted his complaints on the side of it and used it as a mobile billboard to advertise his dissatisfaction. He made his van into part of the omnichannel by using it as a literal vehicle of communication back to the manufacturer.

There is no way to anticipate this sort of outlier behavior, but such actions are usually a culmination of other interactions through monitored channels that have failed. Is it feasible to deliver a literal omnichannel experience? Probably not. But we can all strive to deliver the best continual, connected customer experience possible across every channel, both outbound and inbound.

Originally published on LinkedIn, October 12, 2016

44

The Rise of Vinyl and What It May Mean for Content Delivery

I took delivery of a replacement turntable over the weekend and was soon back enjoying the sounds of my ever-expanding collection of vinyl records. It seems that vinyl is back to stay.

I rediscovered the format about eight years ago when my eldest daughter ignored everything on my Amazon wish list and instead proved that she did in fact listen to her father when he went off on one of his nostalgia trips about the music of his youth. She bought me a turntable for Christmas.

Once we had it set up and were spinning a few of the old records we still had in the house, I had a fairly lengthy discussion with her and her boyfriend (now husband) about how a record and turntable worked and what was so special about the good old LP as opposed to a modern CD or digital download. (Still seems a little funny to me that two, at the time, 21-year-olds had never seen a record being played before.)

With the arrival of the new turntable I've been doing some thinking. Why did LPs have such a cultural impact, and why are they making a return? Records and record players had been around for decades before the sudden explosive growth of music ownership that started in the mid-to-late 1950s and early 1960s. Sure the birth of rock-n-roll had a large part to play, but I thought there must be more to it than that. The following passage by Jonathan Gould in *Can't Buy Me Love* (Gould 2008), his excellent social history of The Beatles, goes some way to answering that:

> Ultimately the attribute that sealed the success of the LP in the popular market had little to do with its expanded capacity or its improved sound quality. Designated as "packaged product" by the recording industry LPs were the first records to be sold in foot-square cardboard jackets faced with glossy cover art, which served as an alluring advertisement for the music within.
>
> This allowed them to be prominently displayed in racks or bins in virtually any kind of store; it also allowed them to be advertised as recognizable products in newspapers and magazines. (Singles in contrast, were still packaged in plain paper sleeves and sold mainly in specialist record stores.)
>
> The LP cover became a companion piece to the listening experience by providing photographs, biographical information and promotional copy.

I started to equate this great piece of social and economic history to the idea of content delivery.

Think about the LP—it still delivered the same sort of content as earlier formats (78s and 45 singles). Yes, it used new technology to deliver more in the same medium, but it didn't find traction with its user base until the packaging and delivery channel changed.

What made it work?

- ► The content was placed in the same location that users frequented anyway—they no longer had to go searching for it.

- ► It was clearly labeled and could be browsed—they didn't have to read the fine print on a label or be an expert.

- ► It was presented along with additional information that gave the content context.

- ► The new packaging was durable and could be accessed many times without degrading, inviting reuse.

- ► Social networks and peer recommendations developed around the ease of accessibility and navigation.

As we all struggle with ways to present our content in new formats and media, creating new content-driven experiences, maybe we can learn a few lessons from the past.

Now you will have to excuse me, I have to go turn this copy of *Abbey Road* over.

Originally published on LinkedIn, December 8, 2015

45

Are You Delivering a Sunshine Experience?

It's amazing how even the brightest ray of sunlight can ruin months of work. Several years ago I was part of an industry team developing a set of standards to define a group of symbols and colors to be used to deliver automotive service information. We worked diligently for several months to come up with the right experience. Then we built a prototype and showed it to several service technicians who all liked what we had done.

Then we visited one technician to proudly show off our work, but he didn't want to meet us in his office. He wanted to use the prototype in a real-life scenario. Outside, next to a big greasy machine! It was all going well until the sun came out from behind a cloud, hit the laptop screen, and made everything we had done unreadable; the color palette we had selected washed out and everything looked the same. Back to square one on designing the experience!

I was reminded of this after stopping to get gas. My local gas station has pumps with a nice big digital screen front and center. Once you have selected your gas and started pumping it plays a mix of short TV news and entertainment clips, along with some marketing messaging. Yesterday the rising sun was at just the right angle to make the screen almost unusable for both delivering the step-by-step instructions for purchasing and pumping gas and for any of the digital marketing designed to engage and entertain me for the few minutes it took to fill the car. A simple lip across the top of the screen to provide some shade would probably have fixed the problem.

Recently a friend of mine tweeted that it's a mistake to only test your marketing content on giant monitors. You should review content on the mobile devices your users will use. Excellent advice, but based on experiences like the ones outlined above I believe that to ensure the sort of customer experience that we believe we are designing and delivering we should also test indoors and outdoors, as sun glare and lighting conditions can affect the experience.

And not just mobile devices; as the customer experience moves beyond the browser, we should also be thinking about embedded screens in Internet of Things connected products, seat backs, digital signage, and other outdoor static screens. The list is growing and so are the environmental factors that can have an impact on the customer experience.

Originally published on The Content Pool, June 30, 2019

46

Good CX Turns Bad in the Swipe of a Credit Card

Of all the things I love about attending industry conferences in Las Vegas, cab drivers are close to the top of the list.

Over the years, I've learned a lot riding in Vegas cabs. On my last trip I developed a whole new appreciation for the early works of Lou Reed and the Velvet Underground during the cab ride from my hotel to the airport. I've also had discussions about a wide variety of other subjects, including robotics, artificial intelligence, how our brains work, the life and times of Marilyn Monroe ,and the problems of staging a low-budget musical.

But perhaps one of my most interesting learning moments happened the day my cab driver's credit card machine lost its connection and stopped working. It was one of those card readers that are fixed to the back of the seat and let passengers swipe their cards for a quick and easy exit. A great idea—until they stop working.

How quickly good CX turns bad

The friendly driver cheerfully said, "Not to worry, we have a backup process for when this happens." At first, I wasn't sure whether he meant that they had thought through various customer experience permutations and had planned for a disconnected card reader or, conversely, that they had a systemic issue and, instead of fixing it, had just cobbled together a procedure. It turned out to be the latter.

I won't go into a blow-by-blow account, but the "backup" process rapidly turned my happy cabby into a frustrated and annoyed one.

The process involved him calling a central number and getting passed from a dispatcher to the finance department to the IT people and back to the finance people, seemingly in an endless loop. At each step, he had to repeat the same basic information, and at one point he had to get out of his cab to find a reference number that was painted on the outside! He had his phone on speaker, so I heard every transaction and exchange, including the ones that included the occasional swear word.

During this seemingly endless process, the driver rebooted the machine a couple of times and got it working himself. He gave me a wry smile as I paid and headed for my flight, but I pitied the next person to step into that cab.

Good CX considers customers *and* employees

As for the backup process, they clearly didn't have one, or at least not one that was accessible, well documented, or efficient. And if any process needs to be efficient, it is one where passengers want to pay for a cab quickly and easily at the airport. Clearly, the cab company had not considered context, customer needs, and the impact that technical difficulties would have on employees dealing with angry and impatient customers.

I'm not sure when exactly it happened, but at some point in my career there was an inflection point when the technology I used at home overtook the technology I used at work. When I started working, the only place where I had access to a computer was at the office. That's where technology lived. But with the explosive growth of personal computers and mobile technology, many people now walk around with more computing power in their pockets than we could have imagined 20 years ago.

With that change has come changes in behavior and changes in our expectations of what our interactions with technology should be. We no longer tolerate the poor user experiences of old. We expect that interacting with the digital world will be intuitive and engaging and that those interactions will provide value and deliver the right content consistently across any channel we use.

Treat employees like customers

Those changes notwithstanding, many companies still expect their employees to use old systems that are anything but intuitive and engaging. And that's a problem, of course, because people's behaviors and expectations don't change when they go to work, whether that means walking into an office or settling into the driver's seat of a cab. No matter where they earn their living, people look for the same digital experiences they have as consumers.

Remember: your employees are customers of other companies, so you should think of them as your customers, too. If you see your employees as internal customers and offer them the same digital experiences you offer to external customers, your employees will be more engaged, productive, and brand-loyal.

The incident in the cab made me realize that there's another aspect to that viewpoint. What about the systems that employees have to use when they are interacting with customers? Customers may make decisions about their potential ongoing experiences with your company based on how easy (or difficult) it is for your employees, agents, etc. to complete their tasks.

Not every aspect of customer experience is a direct interaction; often it's an observation rather than a transaction.

Originally published on CMS Wire, May 3, 2018

47

IoT May Change Customer Experience, But Not Like You'd Expect

It all started with a drip of water. You know—that moment when you open the refrigerator door and feel a drop of water on your hand where you shouldn't. It didn't take long for me to track where it was coming from: a dislodged pipe. At least that's what I thought it was, but I was wrong.

No problem, I thought, the fridge is still under the manufacturer's warranty. So I headed on over to the manufacturer's website and opened the online form to book a service call. It was all going well until the form asked for the fridge's serial number.

Back in the kitchen, I opened every door and peered at every surface of the refrigerator writing down any number I could find. But not one of them was the serial number I needed to pull the warranty information.

When I called the customer help desk they explained they needed the serial number so they could make sure they had the right information about the model for spare parts and to check the purchase date and warranty coverage. That all seemed fair enough. Here is how that conversation went:

"So where do I find the serial number?" I asked.

"On a sticker on the refrigerator."

"And where's that sticker located?"

"Oh, it's on the back."

"On the back? The back that's against a wall and enveloped in custom-built kitchen cabinets?"

"Yes."

That is a great example of the disconnect that often happens when companies focus on the digital customer interaction without considering the actual physical product as part of the overall experience.

IoT to the rescue?

But the Internet of Things (IoT) is going to change all that, isn't it? At least that seems to be part of the promise.

Surely a connected fridge should have been able to supply the serial number from an on-screen menu. Better yet, it should have been aware of the leak and flashed an on-screen warning. Maybe it could have even connected with the manufacturer's customer records, checked the warranty status, and scheduled a visit from technician who would take care of the repairs—and maybe it could have informed the technician of the necessary troubleshooting procedures, activated an inventory and fulfillment process, and ordered the necessary replacement parts in advance.

Yet when you look at the digital features on most "smart" appliances, they tend to be focused on serving as a family communication and entertainment center. They have calendars, display photos, stream music, and maybe support a voice interface for ordering groceries. I could get that same sort of functionality by duct-taping an iPad on the fridge door.

Today's smart appliances don't support the customer-service experience described above. At this early stage of maturity, IoT technology is still more about manufacturing and data collection than it is about delivering an enhanced customer experience.

IoT may travel an unexpected path

We have a long way to go with IoT technology, and I don't believe we even know what the destination is yet.

During a recent conference keynote, I mentioned how these days we expect to be able to talk to things like cars and refrigerators. Voice assistants and voice-activated interfaces are the current example of a leading-edge technology that is reaching critical mass. In a follow-up conversation afterward, someone pointed out that when we first started to talk about voice recognition, we assumed that the prime use case for the technology would involve replacing the need to type. We never imagined that widespread adoption would come when we started to use voice interfaces to ask for directions, check the weather, and order groceries.

That insight revealed a valid point about the contrast between the initial promise of a technology and its actual adoption patterns.

So, is the real IoT-driven customer experience going to be the one we think it will be from today's perspective, or is it something we haven't even considered yet?

Originally published on CMS Wire, November 2, 2018

48

The Man from P.O.S.T.— "The Where to Prioritize Tech Affair"

Despite the fact that for over half of my career technology companies have paid my mortgage, I have always been a long-standing, and increasing vocal, proponent of the idea that in deciding to pursue any business-process change or innovation the technology must come last. In fact I devoted a whole chapter to the topic in my book *The Content Pool* (Porter 2012) (end of shameless plug).

At one industry conference I even ended up getting a quick round of applause during the closing panel discussion when I said that audience members should stop talking about tools and start talking about business need. A sign that I thought meant we were making some headway.

Then a conversation reminded me of a past project that I worked on that had been ticking over for nearly three years and not making any apparent progress. I recalled that the norm on that project was for conversations to quickly get into the weeds about the features, functionality, and development efforts needed around alternative technology options.

When I asked the basic question of what was the project's high-level business objective, no one could articulate it. Was this a project for customer communication or was it a project to prove that something could be done using existing technology? Again, no clear response.

The whole experience reminded me of an acronym developed by the Forrester's consulting group: P.O.S.T.

Forrester created the P.O.S.T. approach as part of developing a corporate social network strategy, but I believe it applies equally well to implementing any innovation or process improvement strategy:

P = People
O = Objectives
S = Strategy
T = Technology

Seems obvious doesn't it. Start with those who have a need, figure out what you need to do to fill that need, develop a strategy to do it, and then think about the tools you can use to do it. You should be thinking along the lines of "We need to decrease the time it takes to get our information into the hands of our customers," not "We need to install Wizgadget3.0."

Remember: if you put the T first, all you are left with is a P.O.S.

Originally published on LinkedIn, August 18, 2015

49

Are We Developing the Dickens of Customer Experiences?

I was in the middle of reading a book on the history of nineteenth-century England when my calendar reminded me it was time to start thinking about my latest column for CMS Wire on the subject of "Tech Expectations," which, given my off-hours reading, rattled around in my brain as "Great Expectations."

If there's one literary figure who dominated not only the artistic but also the social zeitgeist of the nineteenth century, it was Charles Dickens. As well as being a brilliant novelist, commentator, and social reformer, Dickens and his publishers were masters of customer experience.

Charles Dickens: omnichannel pioneer?

Dickens wrote in an era of increasing public literacy; the demand for prose was exploding, and different markets and readerships used different channels to engage with the content. Dickens was an early adopter of the omnichannel experience.

The public wanted serialized monthly magazine installments, publishers wanted a three-volume novel, and after the creation of the first lending libraries, the demand grew for single-volume novels.

Writers like Dickens produced source content that was then distributed across different channels to provide different experiences. However, all of these experiences were driven by the same baseline technology: the printing press.

Unfortunately, it could be argued we've lost our way since then. With the arrival of digital technologies, we have drifted away from the idea of a common source and instead focused on each delivery channel as a distinct entity.

What are our tech expectations when the technology is still too siloed? Because of the way most company budgets are organized, the technology is dedicated to solving vertical business problems, while customers experience a horizontal journey across every aspect of the enterprise.

As long as technology continues to drive individual customer touchpoints, can we ever deliver a seamless customer experience?

How do we reconcile the impact of agile on the customer experience?

Content industry thought leader Tom Johnson asked an interesting question in one of his excellent blog posts: how does the current trend for independent agile technology development teams impact the adoption of content strategy? It's a fascinating question. In the discussion he also tackles how current development trends may be impacting the customer experience.

> **If engineers build separate systems that don't integrate, the user experience also ends up being disjointed and impractical.** [*emphasis mine*] Users might find that … one tool is built on a technology that is incompatible with another. This kind of disjointed hodgepodge of tech is understandable in acquisitions, but few users will understand and be patient with the idea that the single company they interact with is actually made up of dozens of small, independent internal companies that, it has become clear, don't seem to know what each other is working on or building, since none of the products work together. As a worse case, in massive companies, totally isolated teams might even be working on different solutions for the same problem, unaware of each other's existence.
>
> —Tom Johnson[1]

So how do you develop tech expectations that both support the agile spirit and provide the foundations for customer experiences?

Communication is the key.

Development teams and technologists need to be aware of what others are doing, and their awareness of the customer experience needs to cross all boundaries. The old axiom of people and process first followed by technology has a lot of truth behind it and needs to be adopted when considering the customer experience.

It's not only development teams that need to talk to each other; systems need to communicate, too. Information and content needs to flow across bridges between silos. Data, content, and context should follow the customer. Systems need to be better integrated. My tech expectation for the future is standards-based content APIs that are systems agnostic.

---

[1] "Autonomous Agile Teams and Enterprise Content Strategy: An Impossible Combination?" (Johnson 2020). The original blog post has been updated since I captured this quote. However, the current, updated post makes the same point.

The future of customer experience

As in Dickens's time we are undergoing a period of phenomenal social change driven by technology, and along with it are changes in customer expectations. The business model is changing, technology is developing rapidly, new ways of interacting are emerging, and social norms are being rewritten.

However, we all still want to find answers, be entertained, and conduct business transactions as easily as possible at the place, at the time, and on the device of our choosing. That's the future of customer experience.

No single technology or vendor can meet these customer-experience expectations alone. We need to develop a holistic view of customer needs and interactions across all channels, both digital and physical. In that way we'll be ready for voice assistants, augmented reality, virtual reality, chatbots, interactive digital signage, and screens everywhere.

Postscript: The phrase "The dickens of ..." actually has no connection with Charles Dickens; it was in common use as early as the sixteenth century. It was believed to be a contraction of devilkins, or "little devils" and became a more acceptable substitution for the word devil in an exclamation.

Originally published on CMS Wire, July 2, 2019

50

From the Jetsons to Connected Buildings: Intelligent Workplaces

Sitting down to write this article the day after I re-watched *The Matrix* was perhaps not the best idea.

Did I really want to discuss the rise of the intelligent workplace while visions of humans as living energy cells providing power to the machines that had enslaved us were still fresh in mind? We had put the movie on after our youngest daughter, now in her mid-20s, casually mentioned over dinner that she had never seen it.

Personally, I prefer the vision of automation, artificial intelligence, and the future shown in the cartoon world of George Jetson over that of Neo and Morpheus. One company recently re-imagined the opening title sequence of *The Jetsons* with ideas that seem to be not too far away: autonomous vehicles, augmented reality, holographic video conferencing, multi-national locations, robotics, and more.

What once was science fiction is now reality

In his TED Talk[1] on jobs of the future, MIT scientist Andrew McAfee noted that we are starting to see things in the workplace that seem more like science fiction and less like jobs. He pointed out that in the last few years, our machines have started demonstrating skills they have never had before—understanding, speaking, hearing, seeing, answering, writing—and they are still acquiring new skills. Think of the potential when we hook up a personal automated assistant like Siri to a next-generation cognitive computing platform.

> The intelligent workplace isn't just a vision of the future, it's here.

From assigned desks to intelligent systems

It wasn't too long ago that a company's idea of the workplace was a dedicated office building where employees were assigned a fixed desktop location on which rested a company-designated device that contained a suite of applications the company thought employees needed to perform their jobs.

But the world has changed with the rise of a mobile virtual workforce working flexible hours. Employees are on the move, and a large proportion of them are using their own devices (laptops, phones, tablets) to perform critical business operations.

Today, organizations need to present the right data and systems to employees when and where they need them, in a predictable, reliable, and secure manner.

The continuing development of automated systems layered with basic artificial intelligence is helping to satisfy that need through techniques such as machine learning, pattern processing, and natural language recognition. These technologies allow intelligent systems to react to the complexities of the evolving multi-user, multi-device, multi-platform, multi-location, and always-on dynamic workforce.

---

[1]"What will future jobs look like?" (McAfee 2013)

The current state of artificial intelligence is helping build bridges between people and the systems they use, making access to data more intuitive.

Where do we go from here?

Is the next step the development of a true internet of things, where the human sits at the intersection of the digital and physical worlds? As the infrastructure we build and operate has more sensors and transmitters embedded in it and as the world becomes more connected and wireless, the intelligent workplace will truly become a work-wherever-you-are paradigm.

Ultimately we will take it for granted that our personal devices, phones, smart watches, augmented-reality-enabled glasses, etc. will automatically connect with sensor-equipped physical structures. But what sort of activities will we be doing in these connected, intelligent work spaces?

As machine learning and artificial intelligence take over repetitive tasks and remove drudgery from the workplace, will it give people more time to be creative and innovative? Early indications are that it might be doing just that, as the number of start-up companies and new artistic endeavors explodes.

To paraphrase Andrew McAfee, will this be the age of machines that enable creators, discoverers, performers, and innovators to address issues, entertain, enlighten, and provoke thought and discussion?

Originally published on CMS Wire, March 2, 2017

51

Employees Deserve the Same Digital Experience as Customers

When I started working, the only place I had access to a computer was at the office (probably giving my age away there). Offices were where technology lived then.

But with the rapid and explosive growth of personal computers and mobile technology, we now all walk around with more computing power in our pockets than we could have imagined 20 years ago.

Digging through information silos

Yet many companies still saddle employees with legacy systems that have changed little over the years and are anything but intuitive and engaging. Most systems just replicate previous paper processes.

Which brings us to intranets. By a simple extrapolation of its name, you would expect an intranet to be an internal version of the internet:

- ► An easy way to access information located in multiple places

- ► An easy way to find information

- ► An easy way to communicate, share, and collaborate with colleagues, be they in the next cube or on the other side of the world

Unfortunately, this rarely happens.

Most companies have information silo-ed in different systems based around functional processes. Employees have to know which of these multiple systems might hold a particular piece of information before they can start to look for it. These silo-ed systems frequently require different logins and passwords, making a routine task even more complex. And such systems tend to be based on older platforms with outdated and inconsistent user interfaces.

Employee's disappearing patience for poor user experiences

The most common way to try and address these problems is to put a portal in place with a single sign-on. This common interface provides employee news, information, and some basic search capabilities. Sounds great in theory, right? However, most portals still require employees to understand the underlying systems and know where data resides in order to get work done.

Consumer technology has continued to outpace most business applications, especially internal ones. The ongoing improvements in consumer technology have caused a behavioral change. We now have higher expectations of our interactions with technology and information, and we no longer tolerate poor user experiences. We expect our interactions with the digital world to be intuitive and engaging, provide value, and deliver the right content quickly, easily, and consistently across the various channels we use.

Treat employees as you would your customers

People's behavior and expectations don't change when they walk into the office—they look for the same digital experience as an employee as they do as consumers. So why not consider your employees as your most important customers?

They already are customers of other companies, so they should be yours, too.

If you are planning on using the latest in web content management, digital asset management, customer communications, social relationship management, search, analytics, and even artificial intelligence to deliver compelling experiences for your customers, why not do the same for your employees?

Treat your internal customers like your external customers and deliver the same digital experiences. The result will be more engaged, productive, and brand-loyal employees.

Originally published on CMS Wire, October 5, 2017

52

Three Trends Shaping Today's Digital Workplace

Most people probably believe that they work in a digital workplace. After all, if you use a computer you must be in a digital environment, right? But the truth is that most people still work in a traditional, process-driven environment where the computer only replicates or replaces what were essentially paper-based processes.

In a true digital workplace, technology transforms the way we work to make us more knowledgeable, creative, interactive, and efficient.

Trends in the digital workplace

According to research by Gartner[1] the trends that identify the move toward a true digital workplace fall into three distinct categories:

1. Exploiting information
2. Enablement
3. Mobile productivity.

---

[1]"Top Technologies and Trends Driving the Digital Workplace" (Costello 2019)

Let's take a closer look at how these trends and the combination of new technologies, changing expectations, and evolving work practices offer both challenges and opportunities:

1. Exploiting information

Think about your experience with consumer platforms like Amazon and Netflix, which use algorithms and behavior tracking to suggest what products you might like to buy or what movies and TV shows you might enjoy. Now, if companies applied that sort of knowledge to the workplace, they could deliver information based on your personal preferences and online behavior. No longer would you need to search for the information you need to do your job because it would be delivered right to you. But would that narrow your focus? If you only use what's recommended for you, would you ever stumble across—or be inspired by—the unexpected?

The rise of big data and embedded analytics brings never-before-seen levels of information about how businesses operate and how customers interact with those businesses when using their products. The challenge then becomes figuring out how to use that data to gain practical insights to drive decisions that deliver actual value.

Once you have the information you need, it has never been easier to develop content around that information and present it in interesting and engaging ways, both inside and outside the organization. We have moved beyond the time when the only option was a PowerPoint slide deck. Now, the ease of readily available creative applications and technology means that information can be delivered via video, audio, graphics, and animation with minimal investment.

However, a good understanding of content creation and the various types of media is still required to ensure that your messages don't get lost. In other words, just because everyone can now create a video, that doesn't mean that everyone should.

Developing the right differentiation between accessible technology and professional craft is a fine balancing act.

2. Enablement

Part of refining that balancing act between technology and knowing how to use it is the trend toward micro-learning, in which digital technologies deliver the training you need, at the time you need it, through the channel you prefer.

Just think of it: no more sitting in three-day training courses to learn about something that you won't use for six months—if ever.

The digital workplace is about delivering short chunks of knowledge as required. However, this sort of focused training must stay in context and enable the user to understand how the topics fit within the bigger picture of overall processes. Social networks, and even popular communications tools such as text messaging, can be used to distribute this sort of micro-learning.

These tools also drive collaboration across traditional organizational silos as the technology-driven networking and sharing paradigms that we all now use to talk to friends and family around the world migrate into the workplace. As this migration occurs, it raises questions about whether the private and workplace worlds should merge on common platforms or be kept separate, even though they may have common constituents.

3. Mobile productivity

This merging of the workspace into the personal space is not only about the use of social platforms, but also the increasing use of personal devices such as smartphones, tablets, and personal laptops for company business.

Moving beyond devices, there is a trend toward the increasing use of personal clouds, not only for storing photos, but for all sorts of data storage, some of which may be business related. This trend underscores that the digital workplace is becoming a fluid environment both inside and outside the traditional office space.

Managing this trend from an IT and corporate security perspective is, therefore, becoming more challenging. So far, it appears that companies that embrace and manage this shifting paradigm are more productive than those that try to restrict and control it.

The mobile digital workplace also raises challenges for employees as they try to maintain a work-life balance. As the boundaries blur, it can become more difficult to switch off in an always switched-on world. In short, what we get from the evolving digital workplace will ultimately depend on whether we see it as a challenge, an opportunity—or perhaps a combination of both.

Originally published on CSM Wire, June 20, 2017

Conclusion: Just Six Words

Reading back through the 52 articles that make up this book has been an enjoyable trip down memory lane. They brought back thoughts of the people, places, and incidents that provided the stories and inspirations in this book as well as the promised musings and observations on the general state of the evolving customer experience.

The way we work, shop, consume entertainment, and just generally go about our business is changing at what seems to be an every increasing pace as digital technology becomes more ingrained in our daily lives. And at the center of that increase in pace is the way we interact with businesses that use this technology—in short, our customer experience.

Hopefully, I have provided some insights into how you can recognize your customers' needs, give them the content they need, and understand the context in which they consume that content, all so that you can deliver the customer experience you want them to have.

As I was reading through the final book manuscript I was struck by how half a dozen words seemed to pop up on a regular basis, even though the articles were written over a five-year span.

Here are those words:

- ► Holistic
- ► Frictionless
- ► Seamless
- ► Flow
- ► Questions
- ► Tasks

So what makes these six words so important to customer experience? Let's look at them individually:

Holistic

A holistic viewpoint expresses the idea that systems should be viewed as a whole, not merely as a collection of parts. In terms of the customer experience this means that you need to develop an empathetic approach and understand that, from the customer's perspective, every interaction is with one company or brand, not with disparate systems within that company.

Customers don't look at your company as different functional silos, and neither should you. The customer experience should be designed, implemented, and managed so that every part interacts with the next to deliver a complete experience at every stage of the customer's journey.

Frictionless

That journey should be achieved with minimal difficulty; in other words it should be as effortless as possible. Friction in the experience just causes irritation and dissatisfaction,.

Seamless

To be fully effective, you need to provide a customer experience that combines many different experiences, processes, and systems in such a way that customers won't encounter any obstacles as they are passed from one system to another.

Flow

Information about the customer—including account status, history, and interests, including products they use or are considering using—should move in a steady, continuous stream from system to system. This can be achieved using well-designed bridges and APIs.

Questions

Invariably, customers reach out because they have questions about your products or services. This can occur anywhere in the customer journey. You need to think like a customer, so you can understand and anticipate the questions they ask and then provide the right content to answer those questions in the right context.

Tasks

At the end of the day the customer experience is about one thing: helping your customers achieve the tasks they need to complete to make their lives easier.

If you take away only one thing from this book (although I hope you will take away much more), it's this list of six words. Taking note of these six points and acting on them will help you listen to your customers, understand your customers, help your customers, and, in short, deliver a better customer experience.

I'd like to close with a few additional words—in fact, just eleven—that I think sum up everything I have tried to illustrate in *CX Trinity*. If I may borrow from Bob Iger, the former chairman and CEO of Disney, here is what he had to say about integrity and customer service:[1]

> **The way you do anything**
> **is the way you do everything.**
>
> —Bob Iger, former chairman and CEO of Disney

---

[1]"10 principles for great leadership, according to Disney's Bob Iger" (Scipioni 2019)

Topic Index

This index groups the chapters into their main topics

Analytics

Business strategy

Customer journey

Design

Digital asset management

Ecommerce

Glossary

artificial intelligence (AI)
:   Computer systems that mimic cognitive functions such as learning and problem solving.

augmented reality (AR)
:   An interactive experience of a real-world environment where objects that reside in the real world are enhanced by computer-generated perceptual information.

brand equity
:   The commercial value that derives from consumer perception of the brand name of a particular product or service, rather than from the product or service itself.

business-to-business (B2B)
:   A situation where one business makes a commercial transaction with another.

business-to-consumer (B2C)
:   The process of selling products and services directly between a business and consumers who are the end users.

content engineering
:   A specialty that deals with engineering considerations surrounding content, including conversion, management, modelling, reuse, and production.

content marketing
Marketing that involves the creation and sharing of online material that does not explicitly promote a brand but is intended to stimulate interest in its products or services.

customer experience (CX)
A customers' holistic perception of their experience with a business or brand.

customer journey
The complete sum of experiences that customers go through when interacting with your company and brand.

digital asset management (DAM)
A system that stores, shares, and organizes digital creative assets such as images, video, and other media in a central location.

frequently asked questions (FAQ)
A means of organizing information and text, consisting of questions and their answers.

heat map
A means of presenting information that uses colors superimposed over a graphic or chart. In website analysis, heat maps may be superimposed over a web page, with the colors indicating the most used/clicked-on parts of the page.

intelligent content
Content that's structurally rich and semantically categorized and therefore automatically discoverable, reusable, reconfigurable, and adaptable.

internet of things (IoT)
The network of physical objects—*things*—that are embedded with sensors, software, and other technologies for the purpose of connecting and exchanging data with other devices and systems over the internet.

key performance indicator (KPI)
A method to evaluate the success of an organization or of a particular activity in which it engages

machine learning (ML)
Computer algorithms that improve automatically through experience. It is seen as a subset of artificial intelligence.

net promoter score (NPS)
A measure that asks customers to rate the likelihood they will recommend a company, a product, or a service to a friend or colleague on a 0 to 10 scale. It then calculates NPS as the percentage of all respondents who selected 9 or 10 minus the percentage of those who selected 6 or below. (Those who selected 7 or 8 are counted as part of the total respondents, but otherwise left out of the calculation as being "passive.")

omnichannel
A cross-channel content strategy that organizations use to improve their user experience across all points of interaction. It treats all of the channels as being part of a coordinated effort, rather than as separate points.

persona
A made-up description of a customer designed to represent a customer segment. Personas are used in marketing (and advertising) to represent a group or segment of customers.

sentiment analysis
A text analysis technique that evaluates samples of natural language text to try and determine whether the sentiment of the sample was positive, negative, or neutral.

virtual reality (VR)
A simulated experience that can be similar to or completely different from the real world.

References

We use a link shortener because some of the links are extreme long. If you go to https://xmlpress.net/cxtrinity/references, you will find a list of references with the complete, un-shortened URL for each.

[A]. 2016. "What Is Content Engineering?" https://xplnk.com/9k23v/

Barysevich, Aleh. 2018. "7 Types of Content That Dominate Position Zero." https://xplnk.com/plbon/

Costello, Katie. 2019. "Top Technologies and Trends Driving the Digital Workplace." https://xplnk.com/wjp0s/

Gould, Jonathan. 2008. *Can't Buy Me Love: The Beatles, Britain, and America*. New York, NY: Crown.

Johnson, Steven. 2006. *The Ghost Map: The Story of London's Most Terrifying Epidemic—and How It Changed Science, Cities, and the Modern World*. New York, NY: Riverhead Books.

Johnson, Tom. 2020. "Autonomous Agile Teams and Enterprise Content Strategy: An Impossible Combination?" https://xplnk.com/uja0s/

McAfee, Andrew. 2013. "What will future jobs look like?" YouTube video. https://youtu.be/cXQrbxD9_Ng

Moffitt, Sean. 2018. "The Top 30 Emerging Technologies (2018–2028)." https://xplnk.com/g2ihq/

Morris, Evan. 2004. *From Altoids to Zima: The Surprising Stories Behind 125 Famous Brand Names*. New York, NY: Firestone.

Porter, Alan J. 2010. *WIKI: Grow Your Own for Fun and Profit*. Laguna Hills, CA: XML Press.

Porter, Alan J. 2012. *The Content Pool: Leveraging Your Company's Largest Hidden Asset.* Laguna Hills, CA: XML Press.

Rockley, Ann, and Charles Cooper. 2012. *Managing Enterprise Content: A Unified Content Strategy.* Berkeley, CA: New Riders.

Rockley, Ann, Charles Cooper, and Scott Abel. 2015. *Intelligent Content: A Primer.* Laguna Hills, CA: XML Press.

Scipioni, Jade. 2019. "10 principles for great leadership, according to Disney's Bob Iger." https://xplnk.com/yi0qg/

Tapscott, Don, and Anthony D. Williams. 2006. *Wikinomics: How Mass Collaboration Changes Everything.* New York, NY: Portfolio.

Zimmerer, John. 2016. "From Here to Infinity: Personalizing Every Customer Journey." https://xplnk.com/cuf6b/

Index

Colophon

About the Author

Driven to educate, inform, and entertain through content.

Alan J. Porter is a recognized industry thought leader, balancing both tactical and strategic knowledge and a gift for storytelling. He is a regular contributor to various industry sources, webinar host, and podcast guest, as well as an in-demand speaker for conferences.

Alan has written two previous books with XML Press: *WIKI: Grow Your Own for Fun and Profit*[1] and *The Content Pool: Leveraging Your Company's Largest Hidden Asset*[2].

He can be followed at The Content Pool blog (http://thecontentpool.com) and on Twitter @TheContentPool

About XML Press

XML Press was founded in 2008 to publish content that helps technical communicators be more effective. Our publications support managers, social media practitioners, technical communicators, and content strategists and the engineers who support their efforts.

Our publications are available through most retailers, and discounted pricing is available for volume purchases for business, educational, or promotional use. For more information:

Email: orders@xmlpress.net
Phone: (970) 231-3624
Web: https://xmlpress.net

---

[1] https://xmlpress.net/publications/wiki-how-to-grow/
[2] https://xmlpress.net/publications/the-content-pool/